VISUAL BASIC

TIM ANDERSON

In easy steps is an imprint of Computer Step
Southfield Road . Southam
Warwickshire CV47 0FB . United Kingdom
www.ineasysteps.com

Notice of Liability

Every effort has been made to ensure that this book contains accurate and current information. However, Computer Step and the author shall not be liable for any loss or damage suffered by readers as a result of any information contained herein.

Trademarks

Microsoft® and Windows® are registered trademarks of Microsoft Corporation. All other trademarks are acknowledged as belonging to their respective companies.

Printed and bound in the United Kingdom

ISBN-13 978-1-84078-029-1
ISBN-10 1-84078-029-0

Contents

Getting Started

This chapter explains what Visual Basic is, including the differences between the various versions available – Learning Edition, Professional, Enterprise and Visual Basic for Applications in Office. It shows how to create your first application, and explains the Visual Basic environment: the toolbox, properties window, Project Explorer, and toolbars.

Covers

Chapter One

Introduction

The word BASIC stands for Beginner's All-purpose Symbolic Instruction Code. This version of Basic is called Visual because many things can be done visually, without actually writing code.

Visual Basic is the easy way to write programs for Windows. But why write a program? Simply, because it gives you maximum control over your computer. Programs can automate your work, preventing mistakes and making you more productive. Programming is fun as well!

Writing programs can be complex, but fortunately Visual Basic makes it easy to get started. You can choose how far to go. Another advantage of Visual Basic is that it works with Microsoft Office and on the Internet.

There are several versions of Visual Basic available:

*   The Learning Edition is ideal for beginners. Everything you need to create Windows programs is included.

*   The Professional Edition has extra ActiveX components, a compiler that speeds up programs, and better control over databases. This is the version for serious development.

*   The Enterprise Edition is for developing large multi-user database applications and includes facilities for teams of programmers working together.

*   Visual Basic for Applications comes with Microsoft Office. If you have Office or any of its individual applications, you already have a version of Visual Basic.

You can tell which version of Visual Basic you have by looking at the notice that appears when you start the program.

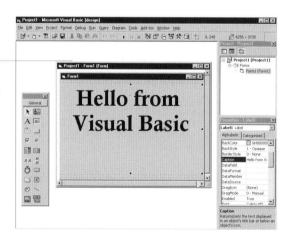

Visual Basic is programming for everyone.

Installing Visual Basic

Although 48MB free space is the minimum, you need to miss out some extra features to fit it in. Try to start with 100MB or more free space. The Setup program will warn you if you do not have enough room.

Installing Visual Basic is done by running the program SETUP.EXE. If you have a CD-ROM version, this usually runs automatically when the CD is inserted into the drive.

Before running SETUP, make sure you have a suitable system. You need:

- a Pentium PC running Windows 95, Windows 98 or Windows NT;

- a CD-ROM drive;

- at least 24MB of RAM (memory), and;

- at least 48MB of free disk space.

The exact dialogs SETUP presents depends on which version of Visual Basic you have, or whether you have Visual Studio which includes Visual Basic as one of its components. You will be asked to choose between a default or custom installation.

When installing large programs, it is easy to use almost all the space on your hard disk. Unfortunately, Windows needs free space for temporary files. You also need to allow for your documents. It is best to keep 30MB or more free at all times.

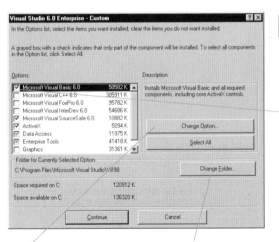

1 If you choose the Custom setup option, then you can click these check boxes to choose which optional components to install.

2 Click here to change sub-options for the selected component (see step 4 on page 10).

3 Click here to change the folder where Visual Basic will be installed. Usually, the only reason to change this setting is if you have another drive which has more free space available.

The main Visual Basic component has several sub-options.

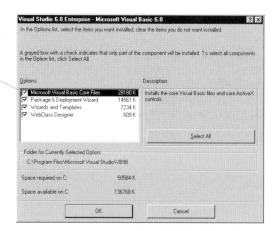

4 Check each
option you
want installed
here.

*If you are not
sure which
components
you need, just
choose the
defaults. You can run Setup
again later on, to install or
remove further components.*

- Leave the "Core Files" checked, as these are essential for running Visual Basic.

- The "Package & Deployment Wizard" creates installers that allow other users to install your applications.

- "Wizards and Templates" speed-up your work by providing ready-made starter projects.

- The "WebClass Designer" is an advanced option for building your own web sites.

*MSDN stands
for Microsoft
Developer
Network
Library. It
contains an excellent online
document set for reference
and troubleshooting.*

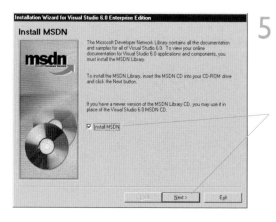

5 At the end of the installation, you will be invited to install MSDN. This provides vital online help for working with Visual Basic. If you have the space, install the full version to hard disk for best performance.

Your first application

To get started with Visual Basic, here is how to create an application in three easy steps.

The secret of VB is using events, properties and methods to bring your forms to life. This chapter begins to show you how to do this, using step-by-step examples.

1 Start Visual Basic and make sure that "Standard EXE" is highlighted in the opening dialog. Then click here.

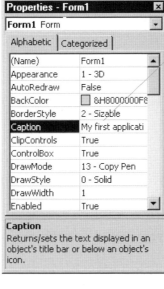

2 Now find the small window called Properties and click in the box to the right of Caption. Type "My first application" and press Return. Watch the title of the form change!

If you cannot find the Properties window, or any of the other main Visual Basic windows, choose it from the View menu. Then it will pop back into view.

3 Click this small right arrow to run the application.

This first application just creates a window. It is a proper window, and you can resize it, move it, minimize it, and finally quit the application by closing it. It may not do much, but you have just created a Windows program!

First look at the Toolbox

Visual Basic's toolbox contains the building bricks of your applications. Using the form from the previous page, follow these steps to try it now.

While you work in Visual Basic, the pointer icon will be selected most of the time. Only select the other icons in the toolbox when you want to place a new object on a form.

1 Click the "A" icon on the toolbox. This is the icon for a label. It will change appearance to show it is depressed.

2 Move the mouse pointer over the form, and press down the left mouse button where you want to position the top-left corner of the label. Keep it pressed down as you drag the mouse down and right to enlarge the label. Then release the button. If it is not quite right, you can move it with the mouse, or resize it using one of the eight resize tabs.

The exact contents of the toolbox vary according to which version of Visual Basic you have and how you have set it up. If you right-click the toolbox, you will see a menu that lets you add and remove the toolbox components.

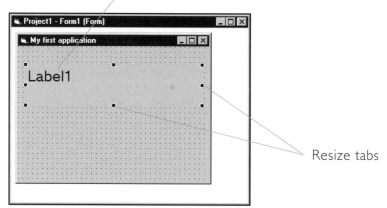

Resize tabs

First look at the Property Editor

Visual Basic's Property Editor is a list of characteristics. Each characteristic or "property" affects the currently selected object, such as a label or button, on a form. By changing these properties, you control the appearance of the object.

Changing the properties of a label

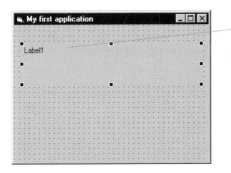

1 Drag a label from the toolbox onto a form. You can use the example from the previous page if you like. Make sure the label is selected.

Every object in Visual Basic has a name. At the top of the Properties window, the name of the currently selected object is shown.

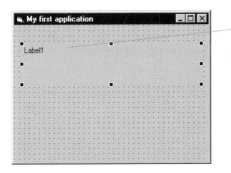

2 Now click in the right-hand column of the Properties window to change some values. Change Alignment to "2 - Center". Change BorderStyle to "1 - Fixed Single". Change Caption to "My Custom Label".

Notice how the appearance of the label alters to reflect your changes.

Getting to know Visual Basic forms

Most Visual Basic applications are based on a form. The form is a canvas on which you paint your application. In many cases, there will be more than one form, and Visual Basic lets you display and hide forms while the application is running. Closing the main form quits the application.

A form is a window. That is why forms have Minimize, Maximize and Close buttons, just like other kinds of window.

Like all Visual Basic objects, forms have properties. To select a form, so that its properties appear in the Properties window, click anywhere on the background of a form.

Key form properties

Icon: small picture that appears at top-left or when the form is minimized

Caption: text that appears in the title bar of the form

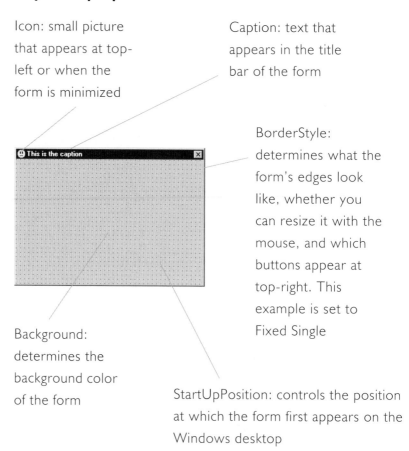

This is the caption

BorderStyle: determines what the form's edges look like, whether you can resize it with the mouse, and which buttons appear at top-right. This example is set to Fixed Single

Background: determines the background color of the form

StartUpPosition: controls the position at which the form first appears on the Windows desktop

Placing a Visual Basic button

A button is one of Visual Basic's most useful objects. Buttons put the user in control of your application. Using Visual Basic, you determine what happens when the user clicks the button with the mouse.

Placing a button on a form

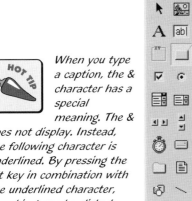

When you type a caption, the & character has a special meaning. The & does not display. Instead, the following character is underlined. By pressing the Alt key in combination with the underlined character, the object can be clicked without using the mouse. This is called a keyboard shortcut.

1 Click the button icon in the toolbox so that it is depressed.

2 Click on the form and drag down to place a button. You can resize the button with the resize tabs, or move it by clicking on the button, holding down the left mouse button, and then dragging the mouse.

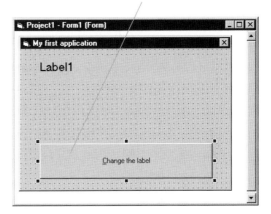

3 Use the Properties window to make the button's caption "Change the label".

First look at Visual Basic events

Most Windows software works by responding to the actions of the user. For example, when you press a key in a word-processor, a character appears in a document. An event (pressing a key) is followed by a response (the document is updated).

This process of responding to events is vital for creating Visual Basic applications. You write instructions to be carried out when a particular event takes place. A classic example is the clicking of a button.

You do not have to double-click to open the code editor. Instead, you can right-click an object and choose View Code from the pop-up menu that appears.

To see how this works, place a button on a form, or use the example from the previous page. Now double-click the button with the mouse. Visual Basic opens a text editor, with some text already entered. It looks like this:

```
Private Sub Command1_Click()
End Sub
```

It is between these two lines that you will write code that will run when the button gets clicked.

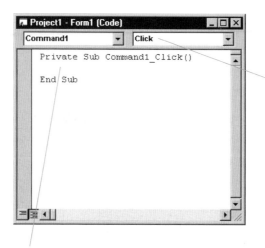

Buttons can respond to other events as well. Drop down this list to see all the possible events.

Double-click a button to open the code editor, ready for you to type in your code.

Your first line of code

To try this example, you need a form with a button and a label.

1 Open the code editor for click events by double-clicking the button.

2 Type "Label1." (not forgetting the dot). A drop-down menu appears. Type "c" and the word "Caption" is highlighted. Press the spacebar, and the word "Caption" is automatically entered.

The coding feature used here is called Auto List Members.

Although it is handy, some people find it annoying. If so, you can switch it off using the Options dialog, available from the Tools menu.

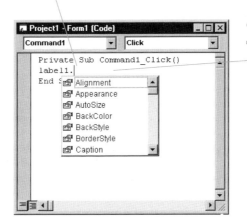

3 Complete the line of code by typing:
  = "I've been changed".

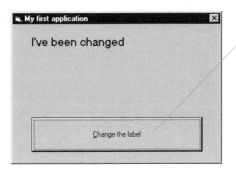

4 Run the application by clicking the Start button on Visual Basic's toolbar. Now click the button. The label's caption changes.

Setting properties in code

Let's look a little closer at the code you wrote for the button's Click event. Here it is again:

```
Label1.Caption = "I've been changed"
```

Now, you could have created a label with this caption another way. If you selected the label, and typed into the Caption property in the Properties window, that would have the same result.

The example on this page shows how you can set properties for alignment and color. These properties are really numbers, but to make them easier to remember you can use constants like vbCentre and vbBlue instead. Visual Basic Help includes a list of these constants.

The code you wrote tells Visual Basic to set the Caption property of the object called Label1 to the value "I've been changed".

The advantage of setting property values in code is that you don't need to know beforehand what the values will be. You can determine them at run-time. You can see this working in the next application.

In the meantime, try setting some more label properties in code to see how effective this can be.

Type in and run this example to show how you can set the properties of a Visual Basic object in code.

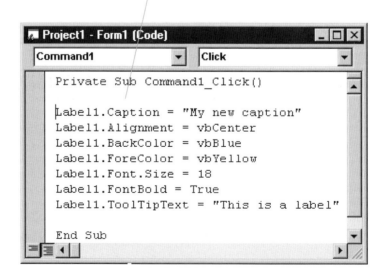

```
Project1 - Form1 (Code)
Command1                    Click

    Private Sub Command1_Click()

    Label1.Caption = "My new caption"
    Label1.Alignment = vbCenter
    Label1.BackColor = vbBlue
    Label1.ForeColor = vbYellow
    Label1.Font.Size = 18
    Label1.FontBold = True
    Label1.ToolTipText = "This is a label"

    End Sub
```

A Visual Basic adding machine

This example is more interesting, in that it performs a useful function. It adds two numbers and displays the result. It introduces a new object, the TextBox.

Creating the adding machine

If you need to refer to an object in your code, it is a good idea to give it a meaningful name. For example, lbResult contains a prefix, lb, to remind you that it is a label. The second part, Result, describes what it is for.

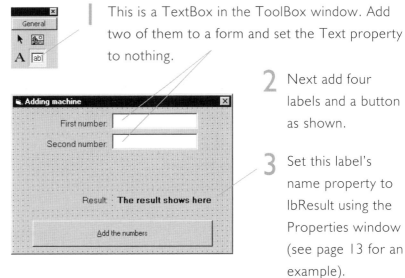

I This is a TextBox in the ToolBox window. Add two of them to a form and set the Text property to nothing.

2 Next add four labels and a button as shown.

3 Set this label's name property to lbResult using the Properties window (see page 13 for an example).

When typing Visual Basic code, you don't usually have to worry about capitals or lower case letters. Visual Basic is not case-sensitive.

4 There is just one line of code for the Button's click event:

```
LbResult.Caption = Str(Val(Text1.Text) + Val(Text2.Text))
```

Don't worry if the code looks puzzling – it's explained in Chapter Three.

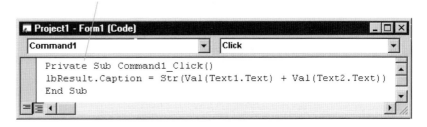

```
Private Sub Command1_Click()
lbResult.Caption = Str(Val(Text1.Text) + Val(Text2.Text))
End Sub
```

5 Now test the application by clicking the Start button. Type a number in each of the text boxes, and click the button to add the two together and show the result.

Dealing with errors

We all make mistakes. What happens if you try to run an application that contains typing errors or faulty code? For example, what if you typed Text1.Txt instead of Text1.Text? In most cases, Visual Basic will halt and display an error message. Then it will show the line of code which caused the error.

When an error message is on screen, pressing F1 or clicking the Help button often brings up further information about the error and how to correct it.

Visual Basic stops and displays an error message.

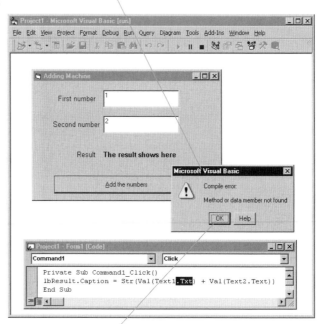

You can write code to catch errors and make your programs more robust. This is introduced in Chapter Eight, Tips for Experts.

2 Click OK to have Visual Basic bring up the code which caused the error.

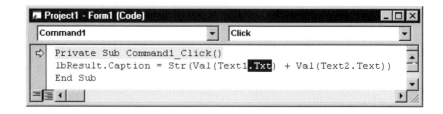

How to get Help

Although it makes programming as simple as possible, there's a lot to remember in Visual Basic and some operations are complex. It is important to learn how to use the on-line Help.

Help through tooltips

Because Visual Basic is very popular, there are lots of other sources of help, including books, magazines and discussions on the Internet.

Let the mouse hover over an icon to show a tooltip.

Help through Visual Basic Help

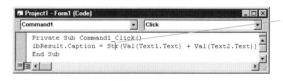

| Place the cursor in the word for which you want help.

MSDN contains a huge amount of information. Limit it to Visual Basic Documentation and then sort by Location to find the key Visual Basic entries quickly. If it is slow, run MSDN Setup again and choose to copy the indexes to hard disk for better performance.

2 Press F1 to bring up help on that particular word, if available.

Help through MSDN

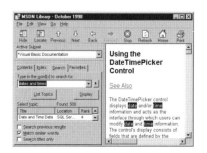

From the Help menu, choose Contents to open the online version of Visual Basic's manuals and other manuals and articles.

First look at the Project Explorer

A Visual Basic application can contain more than one form. It can also include modules of pure code, not attached to any form, and several other more advanced elements. Managing the items in a large project can get difficult. The Project Explorer is a window which lists all the items in your project.

If you can't see the Project Explorer, Properties Window, Toolbox, or other Visual Basic windows, then you can use the View menu to bring them back.

Click here to view the code editor for the selected object.

Click here to view the object itself, for example a form.

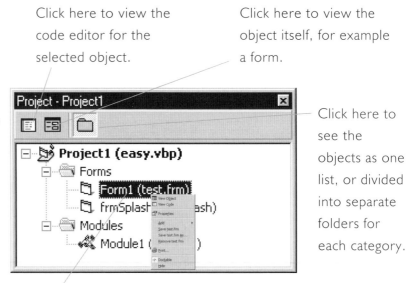

Click here to see the objects as one list, or divided into separate folders for each category.

Right-click an object to obtain a pop-up menu of options.

When to use the Project Explorer

Use the Project Explorer when you want to view an object such as a form or code module. These are not always visible, even when a project is loaded. By using the Project Explorer you can keep an uncluttered screen, just viewing the particular objects you are working on.

If you have a large project, the Project Explorer is essential for finding the form or code which you need to work on next.

Saving your application

Always create a new folder (directory) for a Visual Basic project. This makes it easy to manage your work, for example moving, deleting or backing up the project.

A Visual Basic application consists of more than one file when saved to disk. For example, the simplest standard project contains a project file, with the extension .VBP, and a form file, with the extension .FRM.

When you chose Save from the File menu for the first time, Visual Basic runs through each file in your project separately, asking you to specify its name and location.

For the second and subsequent times, just choosing save is enough to update the files on disk. The exception is when you add further elements to the project, like additional forms and modules.

How to save a project for the first time

If you choose Save As, with a project that has already been saved, then you can choose a new name and location for the main project file. But the other files in the project will still be in their old location. You need to save each file individually, selecting it in the Project Explorer and saving it from the File menu.

1 Choose Save Project from the File menu.

2 Click here to create a new folder. Name the folder and then double-click it to open it.

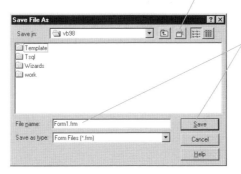

3 Name the first file in the project, and click Save to save it.

4 Repeat step 3 for each file in the project.

Reopening an application

To reopen a Visual Basic project, use the following steps.

I Choose Open Project from the File menu.

2 Find the project file, with a .VBP extension, click on it to highlight it, and then choose Open.

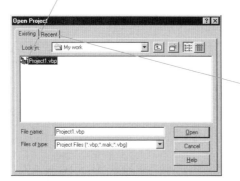

Click the Recent tab for a quick way of finding the projects you most recently worked on.

Opening more than one project at once

Visual Basic lets you open more than one project at once. To do this, use the Add Project option from the File menu.

Having more than one project open can be confusing. It's best to open just one project at a time, except when you absolutely need several open together, for example for advanced ActiveX programming.

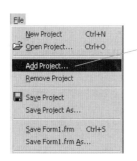

Use Add Project to open a new project without closing the one that is already loaded.

Controls Explained

Visual Basic gives you a wide range of pre-defined objects which you can use to assemble an application. This chapter describes each of the key objects in the Visual Basic toolbox.

Covers

Chapter Two

Controls and methods

The objects in the Visual Basic toolbox are often called controls. Most of the controls represent things that will be familiar to you if you have worked with other Windows applications.

We saw in Chapter One that controls have properties which determine their appearance and how they work. Controls also have events, actions that trigger a response.

Before looking more closely at individual examples, there is another feature of Visual Basic controls with which you need to be familiar – the concept of methods.

If you look up a control in Visual Basic Help, you will see that Properties, Events and Methods are listed. Together, these tell you almost everything about what the control can do.

What is a method?

A property is something an object *has*. By contrast, a method is something that it *does*.

For example, a motor vehicle has properties, like color, model, age and speed. But what about starting and stopping? These are things that a vehicle does. If a vehicle were a Visual Basic object, Start and Stop would be two of its methods. Often, methods have extra information called parameters. These appear in brackets after the method name, and specify how the action is to take place. For example, a vehicle might stop quickly or slowly.

An example

Labels have a Move method which lets you reposition them on a form.

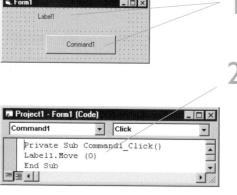

1 Place a label and a button on a form.

2 In the button's Click event, type:

```
Label1.Move(0)
```

Run the application and click the button.

Using buttons

If you have worked through Chapter One, you will already be familiar with buttons. Use buttons when you want an easy way for users to kick off an operation, confirm or cancel a choice, or get help.

Most of your work with buttons involves setting properties and writing code for one event, Click.

The Caption property determines what text appears on the button. Use the & character to create a keyboard shortcut.

Use the sizing tabs to resize the button.

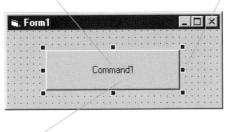

The Font property lets you change the font used for the caption.

For a more interesting appearance, set the Style property to Graphical. Then set the Picture property to a suitable icon or bitmap. You can even specify different pictures for when the button is down or disabled.

Using labels

The label control is another Visual Basic object you will be familiar with from Chapter One. Use labels to display text that the user does not need to edit. You can still change the text displayed in your code, by setting the Caption property.

You can get some great effects by setting a label's BackStyle property to Transparent. Then you can superimpose text on a picture or other background graphics.

Create a multi-line label by setting its WordWrap property to True.

A white or colored background creates a more striking appearance.

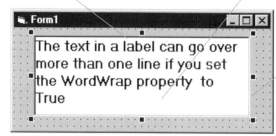

Set the BorderStyle property to Fixed Single for this boxed effect.

How to align labels

There is also a Make Same Size option on the Format menu. This works like the Align option. Using both, you can soon have neat-looking labels.

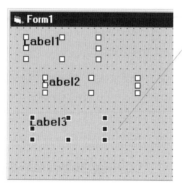

Place several labels on a form. Select all the ones you need to align by holding Shift down as you click on each in turn. The last one you select will be the master, to which the others align. Note the darker sizing tabs on this label.

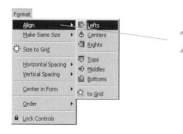

2 Choose Align from the Format menu. Choose Lefts from the submenu to align the labels to the left edge of the master.

Using text boxes

Text boxes are an essential part of most Visual Basic applications. The key difference between a label and a text box is that you can type into a text box at runtime. Another difference is that text boxes can display large amounts of text which the user can scroll through. Text boxes were used in the Adding Machine application described in Chapter One.

Creating a scrollable text box

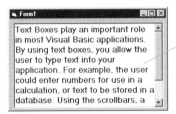

To create a scrollable text box, set its Multiline property to True and its Scrollbars property to 2 - Vertical.

A letter-counting application

This example shows how to access a text box in code.

If you have a long line of Basic code, you may want to break it into several lines. If you type a space followed by an underline character at the end of a line, Visual Basic considers the following line to be part of the same statement.

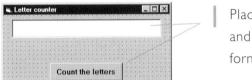

Place a text box and a button on a form.

2 Add this code to the button's Click event:

```
MsgBox ("You typed: " & _
Str$(Len(Text1.Text)) & " characters")
```

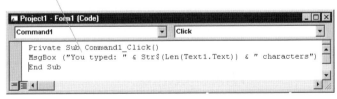

3 Test the application by running it, entering some text in the text box, and clicking the button.

Using picture boxes

A picture box, as its name suggests, is a box which can contain a picture. Less obviously, you can draw on a picture box in your code. A picture box can also be a container for other controls, so you can group them together.

Not all picture files can be loaded directly into a picture box. If necessary, you can use additional software to convert pictures from one format to another.

Loading a picture

Click the picture box icon in the toolbox and place one on a form. Make sure it is selected.

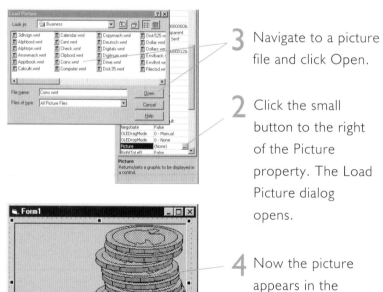

3 Navigate to a picture file and click Open.

2 Click the small button to the right of the Picture property. The Load Picture dialog opens.

4 Now the picture appears in the picture box.

Which pictures can I load?

You can load bitmaps, icons and metafiles. Bitmaps must have a BMP, JPG or GIF extension. Icons have an ICO extension. Metafiles have either a WMF or EMF extension. The advantage of metafiles is that you can scale the picture larger or smaller without loss of quality.

Using check boxes

A check box is a small box with a caption. When the user clicks the box, a check mark appears. Another click removes the mark.

Check boxes are ideal when you want to present a set of options from which the user can choose none, one or more than one. In the example which follows, a pizza restaurant has a form for specifying which extra toppings the customer would like.

The Pizza application

1 Click the check box icon in the toolbox and place three on a form.

2 Add a label and button, setting the captions to some tempting pizza toppings.

It doesn't matter if you can't yet follow the code in an application like this. Visual Basic code is tackled in the next chapter. For now, you only need to know what a check box is for.

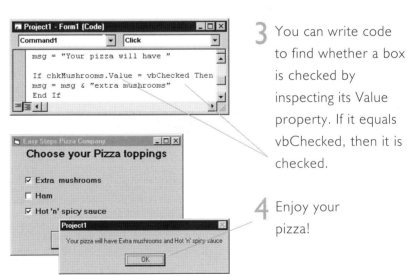

3 You can write code to find whether a box is checked by inspecting its Value property. If it equals vbChecked, then it is checked.

4 Enjoy your pizza!

Using option buttons

An option button is like a check box, but with one important difference: you can only have one button in a group checked. Checking an option button automatically unchecks any others. For example, a pizza can be thin-crust or deep-pan, but not both.

When you lay out a group of option buttons, set the Value property of one of them to True. Otherwise, when the application runs they will all be unchecked.

Thin-crust or deep-pan?

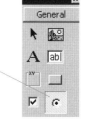

1 Click the option button icon in the toolbox and place two on a form.

2 Add a label and a button and set the captions as shown. Name the buttons optThin and optDeep. Choose one of the option buttons and set the value property to True.

You could combine this application with the previous one, so that the user could choose toppings and pizza type from the same form.

3 Write code to inspect the Value property of the option buttons. If it is true, then it is checked.

```
Private Sub Command1_Click()
If optThin.Value = True Then
MsgBox "You chose Thin crust"
ElseIf optDeep.Value = True Then
MsgBox "You chose Deep crust"
Else
MsgBox "C'mon, make up your mind!"
End If
```

Using frames

A frame sounds like a decorative object, and it's true that it can be used simply for looks. More importantly, though, a frame is a container for other objects. It is particularly useful for grouping objects that work together, like option buttons.

You can check whether a control is in a frame by moving the frame. Controls that are in the frame will move with it.

Pizzas in the frame

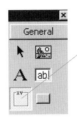

1 Click the frame button icon in the toolbox and place two on a form.

If you want two objects to match, like the frames in this example, select them both together using Shift-click, and then use the Align and Make Same Size options.

2 Set the caption property for each frame to describe its options.

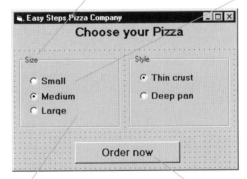

3 Click the option button icon in the toolbox and place buttons on each frame. When placing the buttons, make sure your first click is on the frame. Otherwise, the option button will belong to the form and not the frame.

4 Try running the application and notice how the two groups of option buttons work independently.

5 You can write code for the Click event of this button to detect the choices made, by looking at the Value property of each option button.

Using lines and shapes

Lines and shapes are the simplest objects to understand. Use them to add style and clarity to a form. You can also get special effects at runtime by setting their properties in code.

You can draw lines and shapes without using objects. Forms and picture boxes have methods that let you draw shapes on them in code.

Using lines and shapes

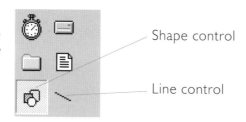

Shape control

Line control

Set the BackStyle property to opaque or transparent to obtain special effects.

If you have several overlapping objects, use the Order option on the Format menu to bring an object to the front or send it behind other objects.

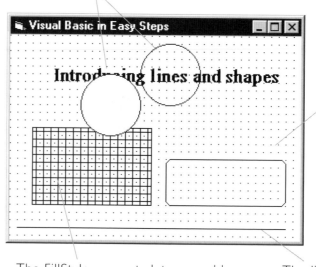

The shape property lets you choose one of six shapes, including a rounded rectangle.

The FillStyle property lets you add different kinds of hatching, ideal for graphs and charts.

The line is one of the simplest Visual Basic objects.

Using images

When should you use a picture box, and when an image control? It's confusing, since a picture box has all the features of an image control and more. Unfortunately, picture boxes are so capable that they use substantial memory and system resources, especially if you use a number of picture boxes together. Image controls are more lightweight. That means you should never use a picture box where an image control will do.

Another method of obtaining three identical images is to place one image and load the picture. Then select the image, choose Copy, and then Paste. When you are asked whether you want a control array, choose No for the moment.

Stretching images

1 To try this example, place three image controls on a form. Load the same image into all three using the Picture property.

2 When you load an image, the control automatically sizes to the dimensions of the image. Once loaded, though, you can resize using the sizing tabs. Size two of the images to less than the full image size.

3 Set the Stretch property of one of the smaller images to True. The image distorts to fill the control. The other image is simply clipped.

So what can't an image control do?

For displaying images, image controls are just as good as picture boxes. However you can't use an image control as a container for other controls, nor can you draw graphics or text on it in your code.

Using list boxes

The list box is one of the most useful and powerful Visual Basic controls. When you want to present choices to the user, a list is more flexible than a row of check boxes or option buttons, because the number of items in the list can vary from one or two to many thousands. Databases like address books or business records often use lists to present the information.

This is the first use in this book of a form's Load event. The Load event is ideal for placing code that runs before the user sees the form.

Adding items to a list box

This example uses a list box, a label and a button on a form.

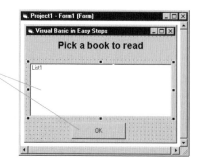

2 Set the list box's Sorted property to true, so that items in the list will be sorted alphabetically.

3 Double-click the form to open its Load event. Use the AddItem method to add items to the list box. For example:

```
List1.AddItem("Alice in
    Wonderland")
```

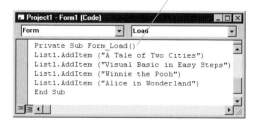

4 Run the application to see the list box filled.

It is no use adding items to a list unless you can tell which one the user has picked. There are two ways to do so. At runtime, the ListIndex property tells you which row in the list is selected, usually by the user clicking on that row. The Text property tells you the text in the selected row. If no row is selected, the ListIndex property is -1.

Retrieving an item from a list box

If you wanted an item in the list box to be already selected when the form opens, you could set the ListIndex property in the Form Load event, like this:

`List1.Listindex = 0`

(Note that the first item in the list is 0, not 1.)

1 Your code should first check the ListIndex property. If it is -1, nothing is selected. If it is anything other than -1, use the Text property to find the contents of the chosen row.

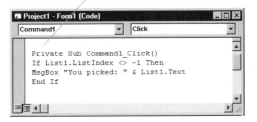

2 Now run the application. If nothing is selected in the list box and you click OK, nothing happens. If a book title is selected, it appears in a message box when you click OK.

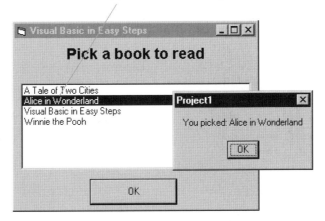

Using FlexGrids

A FlexGrid is one step up from a list box. Instead of just a list of items, the FlexGrid contains cells. Each cell can contain text, a picture, or both. FlexGrids can have scroll bars so you can fill more cells than will fit in the visible area. The FlexGrid features in versions of Visual Basic from 5.0 and above.

If you're not sure what an icon in the toolbox does, let the mouse hover over it for a moment. A "tooltip" appears, telling you the name of the control.

Installing the FlexGrid
The FlexGrid is an ActiveX control. If it is not already in your toolbox, take the following steps to install it.

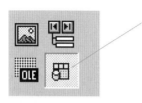

1 The yellow FlexGrid icon in the toolbox looks like this. If it is not there, right-click anywhere over the toolbox.

2 From the pop-up menu choose Components. The Components dialog appears.

All ActiveX controls are installed in the same way as the FlexGrid. Use this page as a guide for other ActiveX controls as well.

3 In the scrolling list, find Microsoft FlexGrid Control 6.0 and click the small box so it is ticked. If you cannot find this in the list (unlikely), click Browse and navigate to MSFLXGRD.OCX in the Windows/System directory. If you cannot find this file, the FlexGrid is not available on your system. Try reinstalling Visual Basic.

4 Click OK and the FlexGrid icon will now appear in the toolbox.

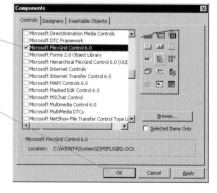

The FlexGrid is so flexible that it can be confusing. The first thing to grasp is that the size of the FlexGrid is determined by two properties, Cols and Rows. These set the number of columns and the number of rows.

Next, you need to know how to set and retrieve the value of an individual cell. This is done with the Text or CellPicture property. At runtime, a FlexGrid has a current cell, identified by the Rows and Cols properties, and the Text and CellPicture properties set or retrieve the contents of the current cell. An example follows:

There is plenty more to learn about FlexGrids. Select the FlexGrid and press F1 to get comprehensive help.

1 Place a FlexGrid and two buttons on a form. Select the FlexGrid and set its Rows property to 10 and its Cols properties to 6. Then set the FixedCols and FixedRows properties to 0. Call the buttons cmdSet and cmdGet.

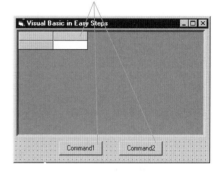

2 The code for the first button sets the FlexGrid's Text property to "Easy!". The second button displays the Text property in a message box.

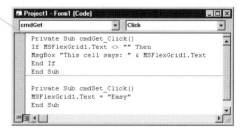

```
Private Sub cmdGet_Click()
If MSFlexGrid1.Text <> "" Then
MsgBox "This cell says: " & MSFlexGrid1.Text
End If
End Sub

Private Sub cmdSet_Click()
MSFlexGrid1.Text = "Easy"
End Sub
```

If the user selects more than one cell, the Cols and Rows properties refer to the first cell selected. Two other properties, ColSel and RowSel, give the last cell selected.

3 Start the application, click anywhere in the grid and click Set. Then click Get to display the new value.

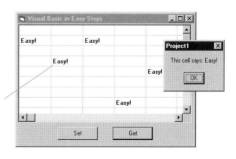

The Common Dialog Control

Many Windows applications need to load or save files on disk. That could involve writing a lot of code, but fortunately Visual Basic makes it easy to use the standard Windows dialog for this.

The Common Dialog Control is similar to other controls, in that you use it by selecting an icon in the toolbox and placing it on a form. It is different, though, because you cannot see it on the form when the application runs. It is there simply so you can refer to it in your code.

Creating a picture viewer

See page 82 for how to install an ActiveX control.

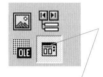

Place a picture box, a button, and a Common Dialog Control on a form. If the Common Dialog icon is not in the toolbox, use the Components option to add the Microsoft Common Dialog Control ActiveX control.

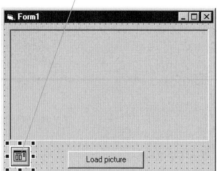

Often you have a choice between setting a property in the Properties window, or in the Load event for a form. It doesn't matter which you choose. It is easier to type longer properties into the Load event, instead of the small boxes of the Properties window.

Open the form's Load event and add the line:

```
CommonDialog1.Filter = _
"Pictures (*.bmp,*.ico,*.wmf)|*.bmp;*.ico;*.wmf"
```

Then add the following lines to the button's Click event:

```
CommonDialog1.ShowOpen
Set Picture1.Picture =_
LoadPicture(CommonDialog1.filename)
```

Now you can test the application by running it, clicking the button, and finding a bitmap file in the dialog.

Once you understand how ShowOpen works, it is easy to use the other dialogs like Save or Font as well.

How the Common Dialog Control works

The Common Dialog Control can appear as a load, save, font, color or print dialog. It can also be used to display a Windows help file. Which dialog appears depends on the method you call in your code. The picture viewer example uses ShowOpen to summon the Open or Load dialog.

When it opens, the dialog uses the Filter property to decide which files to show. This helps prevent the user from trying to open the wrong sort of file for your application. When the user clicks Open, the dialog disappears and the name of the chosen file is placed in the Filename property of the Common Dialog Control.

The title of the dialog is set by the DialogTitle property.

If the user clicks Cancel, the Filename property will be empty.

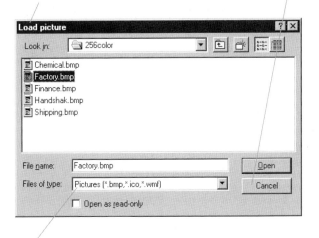

The Picture Viewer works, but if the user chooses a file that is not a picture, it crashes with an error message. See Chapter Eight for how to handle such errors.

The Filter property sets what appears here. This property has two or more parts, separated by the | character. The first part is what shows in the "Files of type:" box. The second part lists acceptable extensions, divided by a semi-colon.

Using combo boxes

A combo box is a one-line text box combined with a list box. The advantage over a normal text box is that the most common choices can be presented without any need to type them in. The advantage over a list box is that a combo box takes less space. Combo boxes also allow the user to type in a choice that is not on the list. The example here is a person's title. Usually this is one of a few common options: Mr, Mrs, Miss etc. The range of possibilities though is much greater, including rarities like Princess or President. The combo box is an ideal solution.

Placing a combo box

You can retrieve the value the user has chosen by inspecting the Text property of the combo box.

I Place a combo box on a form. The other labels and text boxes on the form shown are not essential to run the example.

2 Open the Load event for the form and write code to fill the combo box, for example:

```
Combo1.AddItem ("Mr")
Combo1.AddItem ("Mrs")
```

If you don't want the user choosing a value not on the list, choose the DropDown list style.

3 Try setting the style property to different values and then running the application. Dropdown Combo is the default. Dropdown list prevents the user typing a value not on the list.

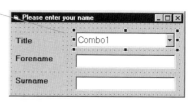

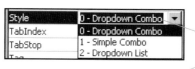

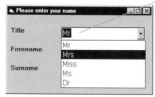

4 To use Simple Combo you need to increase the height of the combo box.

Using the timer

The timer is an invisible control like the Common Dialog Box. All it does is to fire an event at intervals set by you.

Make the butterfly fly!

The following example uses two images, BFLY1.BMP and BFLY2.BMP, which come with Visual Basic. They are in vcr folder of your Visual Basic samples directory, assuming you installed the sample applications.

You can change the interval property of a timer at runtime. In this example, you could have an option to slow down the butterfly or speed it up. You can also move the butterfly by changing the Left and Top properties of the image control.

Place a timer and an image control on a form. Set the timer's Interval property to 200. This time is in milliseconds. Set the form's backcolor to white.

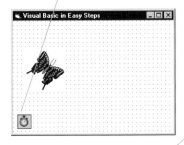

2 Double-click the timer to open the Timer event. This will run every time the interval elapses. Add the following code, replacing the filename in the LoadPicture functions with the location of BFLY1.BMP and BFLY2.BMP on your system:

Don't forget to replace the file names shown with the actual location of these files on your system. If you cannot find them, run VB setup and ask to install the sample applications.

```
Static toggle As Boolean
If toggle = True Then
Set Image1.Picture = LoadPicture("C:\VB98\bfly1.bmp")
toggle = False
Else
Set Image1.Picture = LoadPicture("C:\VB98\bfly2.bmp")
toggle = True
End If
```

3 Run the application and see the butterfly flap its wings!

Using the OLE control

For the OLE control to work, you must use applications that are installed on the user's computer. They must also be fully compatible. Many applications do not work correctly with OLE.

At this point, we have covered all the objects in the standard Visual Basic toolbox except two. One is the Data control, covered in Chapter Five. The other is the OLE (Object Linking and Embedding) control. This is one of the most remarkable Visual Basic controls. It is a container for documents created by other applications. For example, imagine you have an application that creates flow charts, and you want to display a chart in a Visual Basic application. You can do this with the OLE control, which also allows the user to edit it using the original charting application.

An example

1 Start a new Standard EXE and set the form's NegotiateMenus property to False. Place an OLE control on a form. In the dialog which opens, choose Bitmap Image.

Problems with the OLE control can be subtle and hard to fix. If you use it with large applications like Word and Excel, it can also be slow. It's best to use it only when essential.

2 Click on a blank part of the form to turn off OLE editing. Then right-click the OLE control and choose Open.

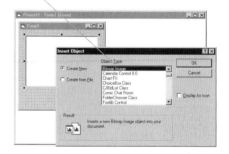

3 The bitmap opens for editing. Draw a picture and close Paint to see it in the OLE control. At runtime, the user can double-click the control to edit it.

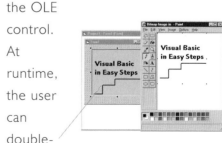

Setting tab order

In Windows applications, the word "focus" describes which window or control is active. For example, pressing Enter or Space when a button has the focus is equivalent to clicking on that button.

It is important to realize that not all users like to use the mouse. Therefore you should allow keyboard alternatives wherever possible. One way is by keyboard shortcuts for buttons and menu options. Another factor is that users expect to be able to move the focus from one control to another by pressing Tab. You need to ensure that the focus moves in a logical order when Tab is pressed. The solution is to set the TabIndex property.

Setting the tab order can be confusing, because when you change the TabIndex of one control, Visual Basic will alter other TabIndex properties automatically. The tab order will remain the same though, apart from the actual control you are editing.

How to set the tab order

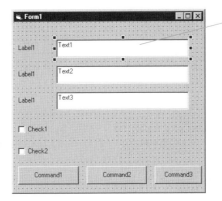

| Place several controls on a form and select the one you want to be first in the tab order.

Not all controls can get the focus. For example, labels never get the focus, so you cannot tab to a label. If you try to tab to a label, you will tab to the next control after the label in the tab order.

2 In the Properties window, set the TabIndex property to 0.

3 Repeat for the next control in order, setting its TabIndex property to 1, then 2, 3, etc.

Other standard controls

There are several other controls in the standard Visual Basic toolbox. They have been left until the end of this chapter because they are the least useful.

Horizontal and vertical scrollbars

DriveListBox

DirlistBox

FileListBox

Before adding the scrollbar to a project, check to see if the object for which you want the scrollbar already has a Scrollbars property. Some objects appear with a scrollbar by default. These built-in scrollbars are much easier to work with than the separate scrollbar controls.

About the controls

HScrollBar and VScrollBar are horizontal and vertical scrollbars. You can use these as a gauge or slider control, or for manual control over scrolling of other objects.

DriveListBox is a drop-down list showing all the drives on your system.

DirListBox is a list of all the sub-directories in the current directory.

FileListBox is a list of all the files in the current directory.

Scrollbar controls are rarely used because most objects have built-in scrollbars. The file and directory controls are not often used either, because the common dialog control does a better job.

Vertical scrollbar   DriveListBox   DirListBox

FileListBox

Horizontal scrollbar

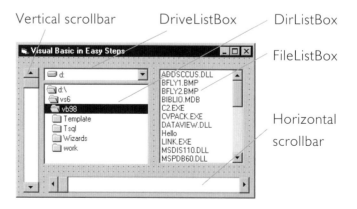

Basic Essentials

Visual Basic lets you do most of your work visually, but you still need to write code that controls the visual components. Such code is written in Basic, the easiest computer language to learn and use. Snippets of Basic have already appeared in Chapters One and Two. This part now explains how to write programs of your own.

Covers

Chapter Three

Start at the beginning

Programs are a series of instructions that tell the computer what to do. Although programs can be complex, each individual instruction is generally simple. The computer starts at the beginning and works through line by line until it gets to the end. Here are some of the essential elements in Visual Basic.

The best way to learn how to program is by doing it. Visual Basic is a safe environment in which to try things out and learn from your mistakes.

Statement

This is an instruction that performs an action. For example, `Beep` sounds the computer's speaker. `FileCopy` copies one disk file to another. Statements are also known as commands.

Functions

These are instructions that return a value. For example, `Now` is a function which returns the current date and time.

Variables

These are words which store a value. For example, the line:

```
myvar = "Visual Basic"
```

stores a string of characters in a variable called myvar.

Operators

This refers to arithmetical operators like "+", "–" and "=". Because it would otherwise be confused with a letter, the symbol used for multiplication is the asterisk: "*". Division is expressed by the forward-sloping slash character: "/".

Objects

Objects can be visible, like forms or buttons, or invisible, like the Windows clipboard.

Properties

Properties are the characteristics of an object.

Methods

Methods are actions an object can perform. For example, Forms have a hide method which makes the form invisible.

An example program

Here is a simple program with an explanation of its parts.

Place a label and a button on a form. Then double-click the button to open the code editor for the Click event.

 The keyword Dim means "Declare". The best Visual Basic programmers declare all variables with Dim, Public or Private. Use the Options dialog, Editor tab, and check Require Variable Declaration. This prevents errors such as misspelled variables, and makes programs run faster.

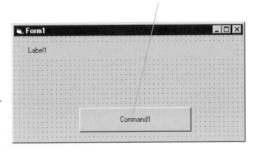

The first and last lines of code tell Visual Basic where this short code routine begins and ends. Sub is a keyword that means Subroutine. The keyword Private means that this routine can only be called by this form, not by other forms or modules.

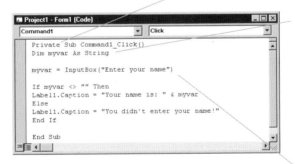

This optional line tells Visual Basic that we are going to use a variable called myvar to hold a string value.

```
Private Sub Command1_Click()
Dim myvar As String

myvar = InputBox("Enter your name")

If myvar <> "" Then
Label1.Caption = "Your name is: " & myvar
Else
Label1.Caption = "You didn't enter your name!"
End If

End Sub
```

This line is executed from right to left. First, Visual Basic calls the InputBox function which asks the user to type in a string. The resulting string is then stored in the myvar variable.

Finally, Visual Basic compares the string in myvar to an empty string. If it is not empty, the label's caption property is set to the value of the string, otherwise a message appears.

Variables and scope

In the example on the previous page, a variable called MyVar was used to store a string of characters. It is called a variable because its contents can change during the course of a program.

How visible should your variables be? The answer is, as little as possible. It may seem handy to have lots of public or global variables, but it makes errors more likely as well.

Variables have some important characteristics. One of them is called scope or visibility. This determines which parts of a program are able to inspect or change the value of the variable.

The MyVar variable was declared in a subroutine. Variables like this, declared in a subroutine or function, are visible only within that routine.

Variables can also be declared in the Declarations section of a form or code module. If you declare these with Dim or Private, then any other routine in that form or code module can use the variable.

Finally, variables in the Declarations section can be declared with the keyword Public. These variables are visible anywhere in your Visual Basic project. Such variables are called public or global variables.

If you do not check the Require Variable Declarations option, then Visual Basic will not report an error if you try to access a variable out of its scope. Instead, it will create a new, empty variable. This can cause a lot of confusion, so you should always require variable declarations.

This is a public variable visible throughout the project.

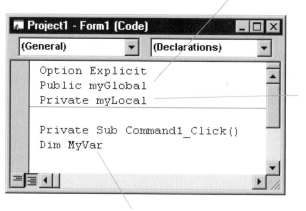

This is a private variable visible to all routines in this form or module.

This is a local variable visible only in the Command1_Click subroutine.

Introducing data types

Along with scope, another important characteristic of a variable is its type. This determines what kind of information (data) a variable can hold.

For example, a string variable stores a string of characters. This is useful for things like names and addresses, but is of no use for mathematical calculations. If you want to store numbers and perform calculations, you need a numeric variable like an integer.

If you would rather not worry about data types, you can use a general-purpose type called a *variant*. Variants hold data of any type. To make things easy, variables in Visual Basic are variants by default. To declare other types of variable, you need to use the As keyword. For example,

```
Dim MyVar As String
```

declares a string variable.

Even variants will not let you do the impossible. For example, you cannot multiply a string by a number. If you try, Visual Basic will report a "Type mismatch" error. Fortunately, there are functions that convert data from one type to another.

Why bother with data types?

Even if you begin by using variants, you should aim to use specific data types as you progress with Visual Basic. This helps to prevent errors, and lets your computer work more efficiently. For example, if the computer knows the data type of a variable, it can work out the amount of memory it needs to store it. That means it can manage memory more efficiently.

Exploring data types

Visual Basic has eleven data types in addition to variants.

If you are new to computers you might wonder why some of the limits here look like strange choices, for example those for an integer. The reason is that computers store numbers in binary, so limits come in powers of two.

String This is a sequence of up to around 2 billion characters. You can also declare fixed-length strings.

Integer This is a whole number from -32,768 to 32,767.

Long This is a whole number from -2,147,483,648 to 2,147,483,647.

Single A floating point data type which holds positive or negative numbers up to around 3.4 E38. "E38" means "times 1o to the power of 38" so this is a very large number.

Double A floating-point data type like Single but holding positive or negative numbers to around 1.8 E308.

Currency This data type is called a scaled integer because it deals with fixed-point numbers that have 15 digits to the left of the decimal point and 4 digits to the right. This is more accurate than   floating-point numbers for currency values.

With so many different types, you may be wondering which to use when. From the computer's point of view, smaller means faster, so use the smallest data type sufficient for every possible value you want to store.

Date Holds dates from January 1, 100 to December 31, 9999. Time information is also stored.

Boolean This is the simplest data type. It has just two possible values, True and False.

Byte This data type holds positive numbers from 0 to 255.

Object The Object data type stores Visual Basic objects. These can also be automation objects from other applications.

Two special kinds of data type are user-defined types and arrays. User-defined types are a group of variables referred to as one. Arrays are covered later, on page 59.

Doing sums

This example program is a calculator. Y[...]
numbers, and the program adds, subtrac[...]
multiplies the numbers depending which[...]

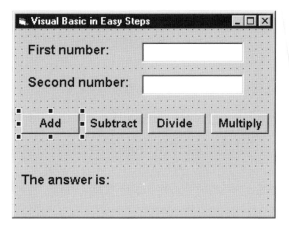

with a blank
form. Place
labels, text
boxes and
Buttons on the
form as shown.

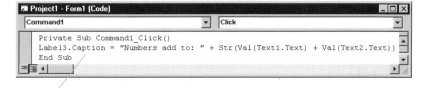

*Symbols like +
and * are used
to make
calculations.
They are called
operators. The four listed
here are the most common.
Sometimes the & operator is
used instead of +, to join
two strings of text.*

2 Double-click the Add button to open the Click procedure.
Type in the following line of code on one line:

```
Label3.Caption = "Numbers add to: " +
Str(Val(Text1.Text) + Val(Text2.Text))
```

3 Type a similar line for the other three buttons, but replace
the second "+" in step 2 with:

- for Subtract
/ for Divide
* for Multiply

4 Run the program to try it out.

...f... Then... Else

Visual Basic's If statement lets you add intelligence to your programs, by doing one thing or another depending on a condition you set.

Putting it to work

To open the code editor at the right point, you must double-click the background of the form itself, not the label.

Place a label on a form and call it lbMessage.

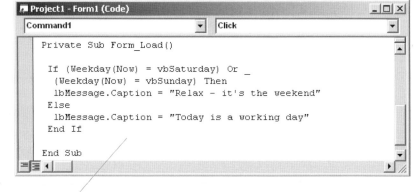

```
Private Sub Form_Load()

If (Weekday(Now) = vbSaturday) Or _
  (Weekday(Now) = vbSunday) Then
  lbMessage.Caption = "Relax - it's the weekend"
Else
  lbMessage.Caption = "Today is a working day"
End If

End Sub
```

This code uses some handy Visual Basic functions. Now contains the current date and time. WeekDay converts this to a number representing the day of the week. Constants like vbSaturday save you needing to remember which number stands for which day.

2 Double-click the form to open the code editor at the form load event. This code will run when the application starts.

3 Enter this code and then run the program:

```
If (Weekday(Now) = vbSaturday) Or (Weekday(Now) = vbSunday) Then

  lbMessage.Caption = "Relax - it's the weekend"

Else

  lbMessage.Caption = "Today is a working day"

End If
```

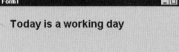

Using For... Next

If... Then blocks let you create branches in your code. By contrast, For... Next creates a block of code which runs more than once.

A For... Next example

This application calculates the annual interest on a sum of money entered by the user.

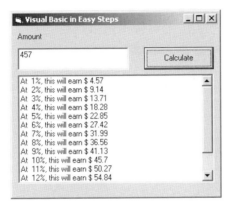

Place a label, text box, button and list box on a form as shown.

Double-click the button and type in this code for the Click event. To use the application, enter a number into the text box and then click the button.

```
Dim curAmount As Currency
Dim iCountvar As Integer

List1.Clear
curAmount = Val(Text1.Text)

If curAmount <> 0 Then
For iCountvar = 1 To 15
List1.AddItem ("At " & Str(iCountvar) _
& "%, this will earn $" & Str(curAmount * iCountvar / 100))
Next iCountvar
Else
MsgBox ("Not a valid amount")
End If
```

Using Do... Loop

Not all loops use For... Next. Two other possibilities are Do While... Loop and Do Until... Loop. Do... While loops until a condition is false, and Do... Until loops until a condition is true.

An example

1 Place a button on a form.

2 Double-click the button and enter the following code for the Click event:

```
Dim answer As Integer
Do Until answer = vbYes
answer = MsgBox("Choose Yes to exit, _
No to continue", vbYesNo)
Loop
```

You can also place the condition at the end of the loop, in the form Do... Loop Until. Then you can be sure the loop gets executed at least once.

3 Run the application and click the button. A dialog appears. If you click Yes the dialog closes, but if you click No it closes and immediately reappears.

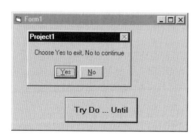

Why are there two kinds of Do loop, when one would be sufficient? After all, you can make a While condition into an Until condition simply by putting Not in front of it. The reason is the clarity of your code. Having two possibilities lets you choose the one that most clearly expresses the reason for the loop. When you or someone else comes back to the code later, to fix a problem or to introduce an improvement, this helps you to understand how it works.

Using Case... Else

If... Then is a good way to create branches in your code, but can be awkward when there are lots of possible branches. Visual Basic has Select Case... End Select blocks, which let you run different code depending on the value of a test variable.

A Select Case example

In this example, note that the line beginning with an apostrophe (') is a comment which does nothing at runtime. Comments are a useful way to make programs easier to read.

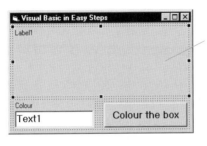

Place two labels, a text box and a button on a form as shown.

2 Double-click the button and enter the following code:

```
Dim sColor As String

sColor = UCase(Trim(Text1.Text))
Select Case sColor
Case Is = "RED"
Label1.BackColor = vbRed
Case Is = "BLUE"
Label1.BackColor = vbBlue
' etc... add other colors as needed
Case Else
Label1.BackColor = vbWhite
Label1.Caption = "Unknown color"
End Select
```

UCase and Trim are useful functions to prevent confusion when the user types in mixed case or leaves leading or trailing spaces.

A better way to choose colors in Visual Basic is to use the Common Dialog control in ShowColor mode.

3 Run the application, type a color into the text box, and click the button.

Using With... End With

The With... End With block in Visual Basic is different from other kinds of block, in that it only exists to make your code easier to write and maintain.

It is a way of executing a series of statements on a Visual Basic object. Instead of writing:

```
object.thisproperty = "Something"
object.thatproperty = "Something else"
```

you can write:

```
With object
    .thisproperty = "Easy"
    .thatproperty = "Steps"
End With
```

This is most useful when the object name is long and unwieldy. Most often this is in programs that control other programs through automation.

An example of With... End With

1 Place a label and a button on a form.

2 Double-click the button and write this code for the Click event:

```
With Label1
  .Caption = "Easy Steps"
  .BackColor = vbRed
  .ForeColor = vbYellow
  .Font = "Arial"
  .FontSize = 24
  .FontBold = True
End With
```

Dealing with a set of values

By now you will have got used to the idea of variables, which let you store values while your program is running.

Sometimes it is convenient to deal with a set of values. For example, you might want to work on the monthly sales figures for a year. Rather than having 12 variables called JanSales, FebSales etc, it would be better to have a single array with 12 elements. Then you can refer to MonthlySales(0), MonthlySales(1) instead. Here is an example:

```
Dim MonthlySales(11) As Currency

MonthlySales(0) = 5242.34
MonthlySales(1) = 3424.43
MonthlySales(2) = 7142.32
'etc
```

Once you have declared an array, be careful not to try to access elements that do not exist. In this example, if you referred to MonthlySales(20) Visual Basic would report a "Subscript out of range" error.

The biggest advantage of arrays is that you can process them in a loop. For instance, add the following code to the same routine to work out total sales for the year:

```
Dim TotalSales As Currency
Dim iCountVar As Integer

For iCountVar = 0 To 11
TotalSales = TotalSales + MonthlySales(iCountVar)
Next

Label1.Caption = "Total Sales: " + Str(TotalSales)
```

By default, Visual Basic array elements start at zero. That means the last element of a 12-element array is numbered 11. If you want, you can have arrays that start at 1 by declaring them in full:

```
Dim MyArr(1 to 12)
```

You can also use an Option Base statement to change the default.

Multiple dimensions

Arrays can have more than one dimension. For example, you could store sales for two shops in one array:

```
Dim MonthlySales(11, 1) As Currency

MonthlySales(0, 0) = 5242.34 ' first shop
MonthlySales(0, 1) = 3424.43 ' second shop
'etc
```

Using Types

Sometimes you need to store more than one value in a variable. For example, if your application deals with customers, you might want to store a name, address and telephone number for each customer. One approach would be to have three variables, CustName, CustAddress and CustTel. A better way is to have a Customer variable divided into fields, so you can refer to Customer.Name, Customer.Address and Customer.Telephone. You can do this in Visual Basic with a user-defined type.

A Type example

This application displays customer details on a form. It uses a Customer variable type. Here is the definition:

This type is declared in a form module, with the keyword Private, which means it is only available to other code in the form module. If you want to use the customer type in several forms, you need to create a new Basic module and define the type in there, using the Public keyword.

```
Private Type Customer
name As String
address As String
telephone As String
End Type
```

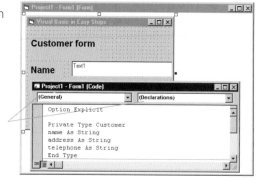

Double-click a form to open the code editor. From the left hand drop-down list, choose General. From the right hand drop-down list choose Declarations. Then enter the Customer type definition as shown above.

Now you can make use of the Customer type in your code. For example:

```
Dim CustVar as Customer
CustVar.Name = "Jones"
CustVar.Address = "4 Park Way, Sometown"
CustVar.Telephone = "01234 56789"
```

Creating a subroutine

When you double-click a button on a form to open its Click event in the code editor, you will have noticed that the code begins and ends like this:

```
Private Sub ... End Sub
```

If you find yourself writing similar code at several points in an application, consider using a subroutine. This makes your code more efficient and easier to maintain.

Sub is short for subroutine. It means that whenever you click the button, this routine executes. You can also create your own subroutines from scratch. Other code in your application can then call the subroutine as required.

A subroutine example

This application continues the example from the previous page. Customer details are displayed in three text boxes. As the application develops, a frequent requirement will be to clear any existing details from the text boxes. Rather than write several lines of code every time that is needed, you can write just one routine that does the job.

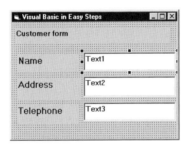

1 Open the form from the example on the previous page, and add labels and text boxes as shown.

2 Open the code editor, and again find the Declarations section. Below the customer type definition, add this code:

```
Sub ClearForm()
Text1.Text = ""
Text2.Text = ""
Text3.Text = ""
End Sub
```

You do not have to use Call when calling a subroutine. It is a good idea, though, since it reminds you how the code works.

3 Open the Form Load event and add the line:

```
Call ClearForm
```

When you run the application, the text boxes will clear.

Using parameters

A powerful feature of subroutines is that you can pass information to them as they are called. This information is called parameters. To illustrate this, and to continue the customer application, the next example is a subroutine that displays customer information on the form.

A subroutine with parameters

1. Open the code editor and find the ClearForm subroutine from the previous example. After the End Sub of ClearForm, add the following code:

You must declare this subroutine as *Private Sub*, because the *Customer* type it uses is private to the form module. Otherwise Visual Basic will show an error.

```
Private Sub DisplayCust(custpar As Customer)
Text1.Text = custpar.name
Text2.Text = custpar.address
Text3.Text = custpar.Telephone
End Sub
```

2. Amend the code for the Form Load event as below, and then run the application.

```
Dim custvar As Customer
Call ClearForm
custvar.name = "Jones"
custvar.address = "4 Park Way, Sometown"
custvar.Telephone = "01234 56789"
Call DisplayCust(custvar)
```

See the next page for another example of using a parameter.

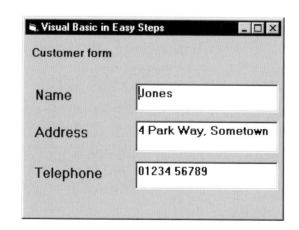

Creating a function

When you write functions and subroutines, you are effectively extending the Visual Basic language. This is what makes them such powerful tools.

A function is very similar to a subroutine. The important difference is that a function returns a value. Functions therefore have a type, just like variables, indicating what sort of value they return.

Converting to inches: a function example

This example application converts centimeters to inches. At its heart is a user-defined function declared like this:

This is a parameter to store the length in centimeters.

This part indicates that the function returns a floating-point number of single precision.

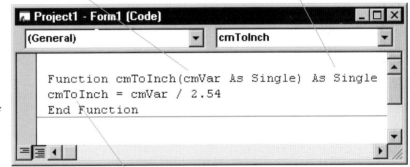

```
Function cmToInch(cmVar As Single)  As Single
cmToInch = cmVar / 2.54
End Function
```

When you have created some useful functions like cmToInch, you can store them in a code module and use them in any project you like.

The function result is assigned to the name of the function. This is what the code calling the function will get back.

Here is the cmToInch function at work. To create this application, call cmToInch in the button's Click event, passing the value of the text box as a parameter. Use Val() to convert the text into a number, and Str() to convert the result back into text.

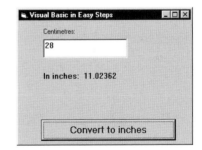

Using MsgBox and InputBox

Look up MsgBox in Visual Basic's on-line help to see how you can control the title, the number and type of buttons, and other aspects of MsgBox and InputBox.

MsgBox and InputBox are similar functions which are used to display information to the user and possibly to get a response as well.

MsgBox can be used as a statement or as a function. In its simplest form, it just displays a message which the user dismisses with OK:

```
MsgBox ("The operation completed successfully")
```

Sometimes you need more than this from the user. For example, many applications ask for confirmation before printing. You can do this by using MsgBox as a function:

```
If MsgBox("OK to print?", vbOKCancel) = vbOK Then
' print
End If
```

Using InputBox

When you need more than just a click in response, InputBox provides a solution. For instance, you might want to search for a customer based on a name provided by the user. Here is how to do it:

```
Dim sName As String
sName = InputBox("Enter a name")
MsgBox ("You chose " + sName)
```

Finally, you can provide a default value for InputBox. In the above example, change the call to InputBox to:

```
sName = InputBox(Prompt:="Enter a name",
Default:="Fred")
```

Now, the name Fred appears in the dialog. If the user clicks OK, "Fred" is returned. If cancel is clicked, InputBox returns an empty string.

Using the API

If you work on a Visual Basic project for long, sooner or later someone will say, "You need an API call to solve that problem." This page explains what is meant by an API call and why you might need to know about the API.

What is the Windows API?

The API is powerful, but it is not as safe to use as ordinary Visual Basic.

You are more likely to crash an application or corrupt memory if you use API calls carelessly. Use the API only if you have to. If you are a beginner, skip this example and come back to it later.

API stands for Application Programming Interface. It is the library of shared code that all Windows applications use for tasks like creating and displaying windows, drawing text and graphics on the screen, tracking mouse clicks, and other tasks. Most of Windows is written in C or C++, which are harder languages to learn than Visual Basic.

In most cases, you have no need to worry about these API functions. You just have to click-and-drag controls and write Basic code. Visual Basic does the work of translating these elements into API functions behind the scenes.

The problem is that occasionally you may need some feature which is part of the API. For example, if you want a form to be "always on top", so that other forms cannot overlap it, not even those from other applications. There is no command in Visual Basic to do this, but there is an API function (called SetWindowPos) which has this as one of its options.

Using the API from Visual Basic

If the API viewer is not in your Add-ins menu, choose the Add-in Manager option. Highlight VB6 API viewer in the list and check Loaded and Load on Startup. Click OK. Now the viewer will be in the Add-ins menu.

There is no problem with calling most API functions from Visual Basic, and there is an add-in called the API viewer to help you. Visual Basic has a Declare statement which lets you identify functions in external libraries, like the API. Once declared, you can often use them like any other Visual Basic function. To try it, start a new project, then display the API viewer from the Add-ins menu. From the viewer's File menu, select WIN32API.TXT.

then Declares from the drop-down list. Now follow steps 1–5 on the next page.

1 In the search box, type setw and then click SetWindowPos in the list so it is highlighted. Check the Private option.

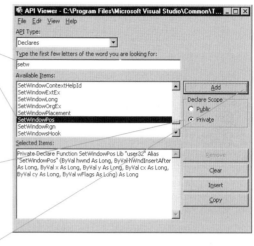

The API functions use a lot of parameters that are really integer numbers. Keywords like HWND_TOPMOST are constants defined so you do not have to remember the numbers themselves.

2 Now click Add, so that text appears in the lower panel.

3 Drop-down Constants and highlight in turn HWND_TOPMOST, SWP_NOSIZE and SWP_NOMOVE. Click Add for each one.

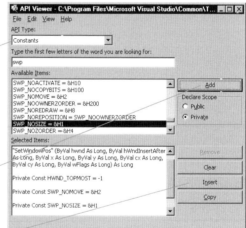

4 Click Insert. When the confirming dialog appears, click OK.

Enter the example exactly as shown, or you may crash Visual Basic. Look up SetWindowPos in online help for more information.

5 Add the following code to the Form_Load event. When you run the project, the form will stay on top of all other windows:

```
Dim lRetVal As Long
lRetVal = SetWindowPos(Me.hwnd, HWND_TOPMOST, 0,
0, 0, 0, SWP_NOMOVE Or SWP_NOSIZE)
```

Printing with PrintForm

Visual Basic makes it easy to create simple print-outs. For example, you might want to print customer details from a form. Here are two ways to do it.

Using PrintForm

Forms also have a Print method. This is quite different from PrintForm. Print is a way of printing on the form, not printing to the printer.

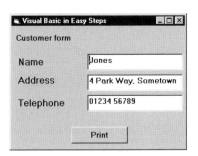

This is the customer display form, described earlier in this chapter. Notice that a Print button has been added. There are two ways to make this work. The first and easiest is to call the form's PrintForm method. Simply add this line to the Print button's Click event:

```
Me.PrintForm
```

Graphics on a form only print if the form's AutoRedraw property is True.

When you use PrintForm, Visual Basic sends an image of the form to the printer. If there are several printers available, Visual Basic will use the one set as the Windows default.

Problems with PrintForm

There are several problems with PrintForm:

- Graphics only print if the form's AutoRedraw property is set to True (False is the default).

- The print quality is at the resolution of the screen, and can look "blocky" on a good-quality printer.

- Often the design of the form is not ideal for a printed page.

The solution is to use the Printer object instead. This is described on the next page.

Printing with the Printer Object

The Printer object is a built-in object you can refer to in your code. You don't have to take any special steps to make the printer object available; it will just work as long as the user has a functioning printer attached.

Using the Printer Object

Here is some code that, like the last example, will print the customer details from a form:

```
Printer.Print "Customer details"
Printer.Print ' leave a space
Printer.Print "Name: " + Text1.Text
Printer.Print "Address: " + Text2.Text
Printer.Print "Telephone: " + Text3.Text
Printer.EndDoc
```

It is not until EndDoc that the output actually gets sent to the printer. Up until then, you can cancel the print with the KillDoc method.

Problems and suggestions

The problem with a simple routine like the above is that it will look very plain. The font used will be the default font. If you send a line of text longer than fits on the page, it will just be cut off. In other words, it needs a lot of refinement before you can get really professional results.

You can set the printer font, by adjusting the Font property. For example:

```
Printer.Font = "Arial"
Printer.FontSize = 12
```

If you are not sure which fonts will be available, use Arial, Courier or Times New Roman. These come with Windows and are almost always installed.

You can also check that the font exists, by looking at the Fonts property, a collection of all available fonts. You can detect the size of the paper using the printer's Height and Width properties, print graphics using graphics methods, and position the output precisely using the CurrentX and CurrentY properties. To make long lines of text wrap round, you need to measure them and break them up in your code. As you can tell, making full use of the printer object is complex and beyond the scope of this book. Stick to simple usage until you are ready to tackle advanced programming with Visual Basic.

Visual Basic Tools

Visual Basic's tools and wizards are powerful but can be confusing at first. This chapter describes essential features like the menu editor, the debugger, and the reference manager. It also explains how to set Visual Basic options so you can work the way you want.

Covers

Chapter Four

Creating a menu

Most Windows applications use a menu to give users full control. It is easy to add a menu bar to a Visual Basic project.

All menu items must have a name. Otherwise, Visual Basic will not let you use the menu.

1 Start a new project and choose Menu Editor from the Tools menu.

2 Type the text for each menu item in the Caption box. Then type a name for the menu (the name should remind you which menu item it describes). Then click Next to add the menu item to the list. Do this three times, to create menu items for File, Edit and Help.

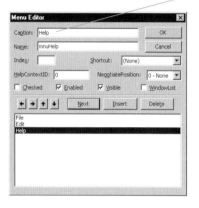

If you put an "&" character before a letter in a menu caption, it will make a shortcut key. When the menu is displayed, the shortcut letter will be underlined.

3 Next, highlight the Edit menu item and click Insert. A new, blank item appears above it. Select it and give it the caption "Open". Now click the small right-pointing arrow. The Open menu item will be indented from the list. Click OK to close the menu editor.

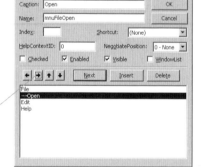

You can use the small up and down buttons to change the order of the menu items in the list.

4 When you run the application, notice that the three main entries run along the top of the form, making a menu bar. The Open entry is on the File drop-down menu. That is because it was indented in the menu editor.

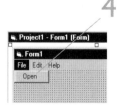

Customizing a menu

There are several ways in which Visual Basic menus can be customized. This is done through options in the menu editor.

The Enabled and Visible options control how the menu item behaves. If Enabled is not checked, the menu will be grayed out and will not trigger any action. If Visible is not checked, the menu will not appear at all.

There is a difference between a shortcut key selected from the drop-down list, and creating a shortcut key with the "&" character. The first kind is more powerful, since it immediately carries out the menu action. The second kind only operates when actually navigating a menu. The menu first has to be activated with Alt.

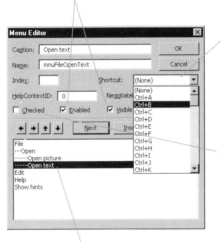

I Choose a shortcut key to have the menu action performed whenever the key combination is pressed.

2 Choose the Checked option to create a menu which has a tick mark to show an option is selected.

3 Create a submenu by indenting the menu item further.

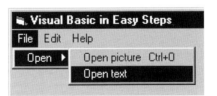

This menu features a submenu and a shortcut key combination.

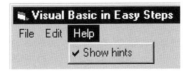

This is a checked menu.

Creating a pop-up menu

Windows applications often use a pop-up menu, which usually appears as a result of clicking the right mouse button. The menu which appears usually varies according to what object the mouse is over when the right button is pressed. Follow these steps:

You cannot use the Click event to detect a right-mouse click. Click fires whichever button is clicked. Instead, use the MouseDown event.

1 Open the menu editor and create a new menu. In this example it is called mnuPopup. Uncheck its Visible property. Then add several indented items below it. These should have Visible ticked as normal.

The key line in this code looks unusual at first. The code:

        If Button
    And vbRightButton

uses a technique called bitwise comparison to detect whether the Button parameter has the vbRightButton bit set.

2 Place a picture box on the form. Double-click the picture box to open the code editor. From the drop-down list at the top right, choose MouseDown. This creates a MouseDown procedure. Enter the three lines of code shown.

3 Run the application and click the right mouse over the picture. The menu you defined opens as a pop-up menu.

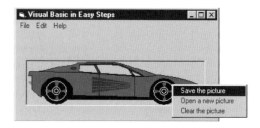

Making a menu work

The menus you have created look nice, but they do not actually do anything yet. This page explains how to write code that runs when the menu option is chosen.

After defining a menu in the menu editor, close it so that you see the new menu on the form. Then select a menu option just as you would if the application were running. This opens the code editor at the Click event for the menu item chosen.

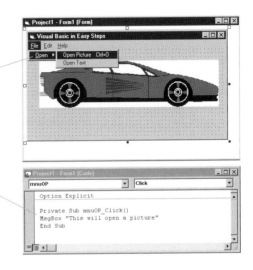

You can use the technique described here to find any Visual Basic code, or to create new procedures and functions. It is sometimes more convenient than double-clicking an object.

If you designed an invisible menu, such as a pop-up menu, then you will not be able to use the technique described above. Instead, double-click anywhere on the form to open the code editor. In the drop-down list at the top-right, find the menu item you need. Visual Basic will automatically open the Click event for that menu.

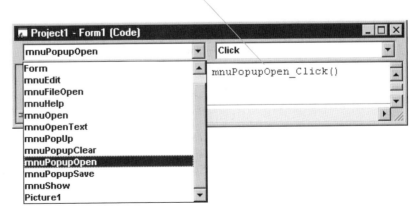

Changing menus at runtime

The best Windows applications protect the user from options that are irrelevant or impossible. For example, a word-processor should not have a Save option when no document is open. The most common technique is to disable or hide menu options according to the current state of the application.

This example uses the application described in "Creating a pop-up menu" on page 72. When you right-click a picture, a pop-up menu appears which includes Save and Clear options. If there is no picture present, the Save and Clear options should be disabled.

This code will only run if your menu items have the names shown. You can change the names of menu items by opening the menu editor.

The secret is to write code that changes the Enabled property of a menu between True and False. For example, here is how you can amend the code for the MouseDown event to enable or disable the Save and Clear options:

Open this code by double-clicking the picture box and finding MouseDown from the right-hand drop-down list.

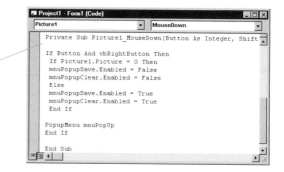

```
Private Sub Picture1_MouseDown(Button As Integer, Shift

If Button And vbRightButton Then
  If Picture1.Picture = 0 Then
  mnuPopupSave.Enabled = False
  mnuPopupClear.Enabled = False
  Else
  mnuPopupSave.Enabled = True
  mnuPopupClear.Enabled = True
  End If

PopupMenu mnuPopUp
End If

End Sub
```

You can also hide menu items completely by setting the visible property to False.

When you run the application and right-click the picture, the pop-up menu will show disabled Save and Clear options if there is no picture loaded. Otherwise, the options will be enabled.

Another useful property is Checked. By changing this from False to True, you can have a tick appear beside a menu. This lets users see at a glance whether a particular option is selected or not, without having to open a dialog box.

Creating a toolbar

Visual Basic includes a toolbar control to make it easy to add toolbars to your application. It works together with another control called an ImageList.

The Learning Edition of Visual Basic may not have a Toolbar control. You can still create a toolbar using a picture box and image controls.

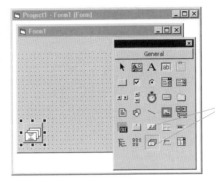

1 Right-click the Toolbox, choose components, and check Microsoft Windows Common Controls 6.0. Then select the Toolbar from the toolbox and place it on a form. Next, add an Image List control.

A range of suitable images is supplied with Visual Basic. On most systems they are in the Program Files directory on the C drive, in the Microsoft Visual Studio/Common /Graphics section.

2 Right-click the image control on the form, and choose the Images tab. Click Insert Picture and select some picture files to add to the toolbar. Click Open to add them. You can select more than one at a time by holding down Shift or Ctrl.

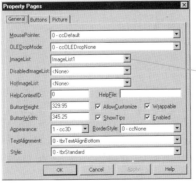

3 Right-click the toolbar control on the form, and choose the General tab. Click the small drop-down button for ImageList, and choose the name for the ImageList control on the form. Keep this dialog open for the next step.

This operation is very simple if you keep the images in the ImageList in the same order as the buttons on the toolbar.

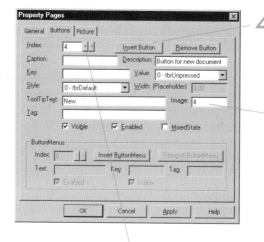

4 For each button you want in the toolbar, first click Insert Button. Then change the image number to match the index of the right image in the ImageList.

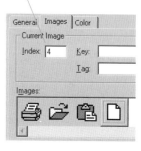

Click these arrows to switch back and forth between buttons. Click Apply, or close the dialog with OK to save the changes.

The toolbar control has a number of other features. See online Help for information about further options available.

5 To write code for the toolbar, double-click to open its ButtonClick event. There is only one ButtonClick event for the whole toolbar. Use the Button parameter to detect which one was clicked. Use a Select Case statement to run the right code for each button.

6 Run the application to see the toolbar in action.

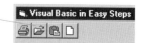

Working with the code editor

As you work with Visual Basic, much of your time is spent writing and editing code in the code editor. Although it looks simple, this editor has many features which make your work easier.

If you find these features annoying, they can be turned off using the Options dialog, on the Tools menu.

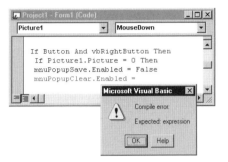

Syntax Checking

When you come to the end of a line of code and press Enter, Visual Basic detects syntax errors like an "=" sign with nothing after it.

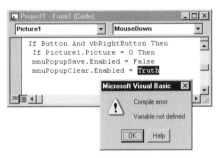

Compile before run

If you choose "Start with full compile" from the Run menu, Visual Basic will detect spelling errors and mistakes that make it impossible to compile the code.

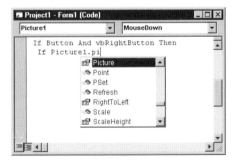

Quick Info and AutoList members

As you type a dot, a list of properties and methods pops up. Select the right one and press Tab to complete it.

You can summon Quick Info at any time by right-clicking over a word in the code editor and choosing Quick Info from the pop-up menu.

Quick Info also pops up automatically, showing the right parameters for a function.

```
MsgBox (
MsgBox(Prompt, [Buttons As VbMsgBoxStyle = vbOKOnly], [Title], [HelpFile],
[Context]) As VbMsgBoxResult
```

Introducing the debugger

Most programs do not work as you expect the first time you run them. The reason is that computers are completely literal-minded, and just one letter wrong in 1000 lines of code is enough to stop your program working. Other problems are programs that work, but too slowly; or programs that work most of the time, but occasionally produce wrong results.

Normally, the program code is invisible when it is running, but the key feature of the debugger is that it lets you watch your program run line-by-line. You can also pause the program to inspect the current value of variables.

Basic debugging

What if your program is in an infinite loop? Press Ctrl+Break to stop it running and open the debugger.

1 To watch your program run line-by-line, start it running by choosing Step Into from the Debug menu.

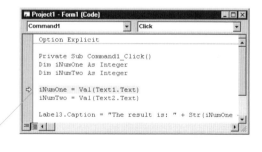

2 As soon as the program hits some Visual Basic code, the code window opens with a small arrow showing which line is active.

Press F8 to run each line, or F5 to stop debugging.

More about debugging

When the debugger is active there are several ways to get information about your program.

Rest the mouse pointer over a variable to see its current value.

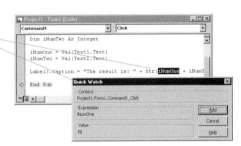

Highlight a word or expression and press Shift+F9 to open the Quick Watch window.

The Immediate window lets you try out commands and test or change the value of variables while your program runs. If the Immediate window is not visible, select it from the View menu.

Type "?" followed by a variable or expression to see its value. Use "=" to assign a new value to a variable.

To add a variable to the Watches window, select it and then drag it from the code window. Alternatively, right-click the Watches window and choose Add Watch.

The Locals window lists all the variables which are local to the current procedure or function in a list, with their values. The Watches window lets you choose which of your program's variables you want to keep an eye on, and displays them with their values, updated automatically as the program runs. Both are on the View menu.

The Locals window

The Watches window

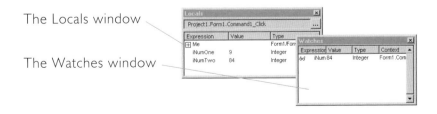

Using breakpoints

When a program is of any significant size, stepping through all the code takes too long, especially when most of it is working fine.

Visual Basic lets you set breakpoints, so that the program runs as normal until it hits the line you have marked. At that moment, the program pauses and the debugger opens.

How to set a breakpoint

You can also set and remove breakpoints by pressing F9.

To set a breakpoint, open the code editor. Click with the mouse in the left margin. A dot appears, showing that a breakpoint is set. When you run the code it will pause there. To remove the breakpoint, click on the dot.

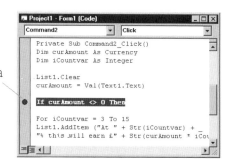

A feature called Step Out is similar to Step Over. Step Out runs the remaining code in the current procedure without stepping, and resumes stepping at the next opportunity. To use Step Out press Shift+Ctrl+F8, or choose it from the Debug menu.

Using Step Over

Imagine you have defined your own Visual Basic functions. If you are stepping through a procedure which uses your user-defined function, then Visual Basic will follow the code from the procedure, into the function, and out again. This nesting can become deep as one function calls another. If you want to concentrate on the code in the current procedure, you can use Step Over or press Shift+F8 to move through the code. Then, Visual Basic runs the code in the function without stepping through it.

This code is about to call a user-defined function. Press F8 to step through the function, or Shift+F8 to run it without stepping through line-by-line.

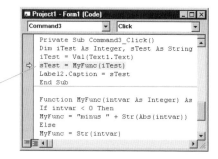

Tracking down errors

Some programs compile and run fine, but fail with an error when certain actions are performed. When that happens, Visual Basic pops up an error dialog. There are several options.

If you or another user is running the application outside the development environment, and an error like this occurs, a less friendly dialog appears. Then the application exits. You can prevent this from happening by using error handlers, described on pages 160–161.

Click End to terminate the application immediately.

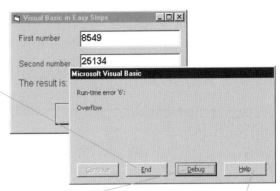

Click Debug to open the debugger on the line where the error occurred. If the error is just in that line, you can fix it and press F5 to continue running the application.

This particular error is caused by summing two integers which together total over 32,767. The problem can be solved by changing the variables to the Long data type.

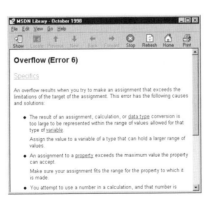

Click Help to display more information about the error.

Managing ActiveX controls

One of the best features of Visual Basic is that you can add ActiveX components to your project. All versions of Visual Basic come with a selection of ActiveX controls, and others can be obtained separately.

What is an ActiveX control?

If you can work with standard Visual Basic objects like buttons and list boxes, then you can work with ActiveX controls. You use them in just the same way. They appear on the toolbox, you can place them on a form, and control them by setting properties and calling methods. Some ActiveX controls are as simple as standard Visual Basic objects, while others are packed with features.

Using the Component Manager

To use an ActiveX control, you first have to install it on the Visual Basic toolbox. Here is how to do it.

You will probably find ActiveX controls on your system which you cannot use in Visual Basic. Some ActiveX controls are installed for runtime use only. To use them in Visual Basic you have to buy a licence. Others are not designed to work with Visual Basic. Sometimes a faulty Windows installation prevents controls from working properly.

Right-click the toolbox and choose Components... from the pop-up menu.

2 The Controls tab shows a list of all the ActiveX controls installed on your system. For example, check the Microsoft FlexGrid Control. Then click OK.

3 The new ActiveX control appears at the bottom of the toolbox. You can now use it in the same way as other controls on the toolbox.

Using the Add-in Manager

Another way of extending Visual Basic's powers is by the use of add-ins. Unlike ActiveX controls, add-ins are not used at runtime. Instead, they enhance the Visual Basic development environment, either adding new features or making existing features easier to use.

Using the Add-in Manager

The list of available Add-ins depends on which version of Visual Basic you have installed. You can also purchase Add-ins as separate products.

1 Choose Add-in Manager from the Add-in menu. A list of add-ins appears. Click on one you want to install.

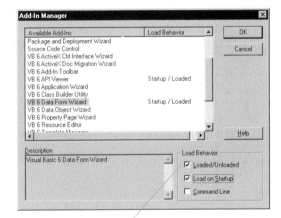

2 Check "Loaded" to install it for this session. Check "Load on Startup" to have it always loaded. "Command Line" is for advanced use – see Help.

3 To use the Add-in, choose it from the Add-in menu. The exact functions of the Add-in vary greatly. Some may add extra toolbars or other menu options to Visual Basic. Others act like a wizard, automating a common task.

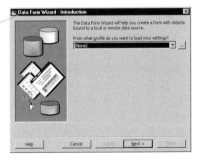

Explaining the Reference Manager

Some advanced Visual Basic applications use objects in other programs as if they were objects in Visual Basic itself.

An example is when a Visual Basic program automatically fills in values in an Excel spreadsheet. From Visual Basic, you can not only put information into spreadsheet cells, but also format the cells, perform calculations, and open, close or print the worksheets.

You don't need to use the Reference Manager to get started with Visual Basic. This information will be useful when you want to integrate your application with other products like Word and Excel.

To do this efficiently, Visual Basic needs to load a description of the objects found in Excel, complete with all their properties and methods. This also enables Visual Basic to check the code that controls Excel objects to see if it is valid. These object descriptions are called "type libraries" and they are loaded by means of the Reference Manager.

Another use of the Reference Manager is when you have written Visual Basic programs that are designed to be used by other Visual Basic programs. You can create programs that have their own type libraries, like Excel, and load these libraries through the Reference Manager.

As with Add-ins and ActiveX controls, the list of available references depends on what else is installed on your system.

The Reference Manager is used to add or remove references to type libraries. To use it, check the required type libraries and click OK.

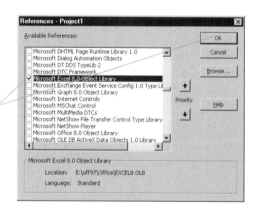

When you add and remove references you will not immediately notice any difference. It does change what you can do in your Visual Basic code, though. For example, once you have included a reference to Excel, you can use a line like:

```
Dim xl As Excel.Application
```

Setting Visual Basic options

The Options dialog is found in the Tools menu. Using Options, you can change the behavior of Visual Basic to your liking. For example, the Editor tab controls the extra features of the code editor like Auto Syntax check.

Visual Basic's default options are good ones. If you change them, change them one at a time so you can easily go back to the default if you want.

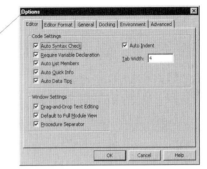

Use the Options dialog to customize Visual Basic to suit the way you work.

SDI and MDI mode

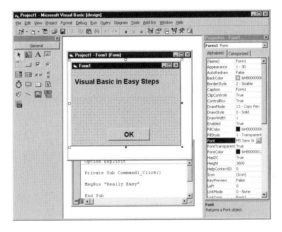

One handy option is Save Changes, on the Environment tab. Set it to Save when a program starts, so that you will not lose your work in the event of a power failure or software crash.

One important option is on the Advanced tab. In MDI (Multiple Document Interface) mode, windows can be docked. Maximized windows just fill the space in the middle.

In SDI (Single Document Interface) mode, all the windows float freely. Maximized windows fill nearly the whole screen. Older versions of Visual Basic only work in SDI mode.

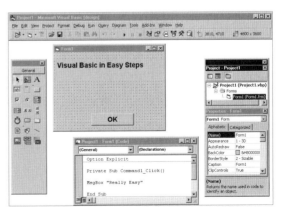

Setting project properties

The Tools>Options dialog changes the behavior of Visual Basic, irrespective of which project you are working on. There are other important options which only affect the current project. These are set from the Project Properties dialog. You can find this at the bottom of the Project menu, or by right-clicking the project name in the Project Explorer.

Using project properties

Many of the options in Project Properties are for creating ActiveX components and are beyond the scope of this book. Some options are more generally useful, though. Here are two that you should know about.

You can learn more about creating stand-alone Visual Basic programs on page 89.

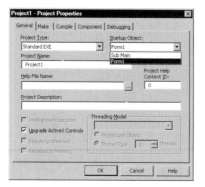

If your project has more than one form, you can choose which one appears on startup by selecting the Startup Object. Another option is Sub Main, which means Visual Basic will look for a procedure called Main in a code module, and start by running that. You can display the forms you need from Sub Main, or create applications that do not use forms.

When you want to create a stand-alone Visual Basic program, you can compile it to p-code or native code. This option is on the Compile tab. P-code executables are smaller but run slower. Native code executables are larger, but may be faster if you have a lot of Visual Basic code to run. Forms and ActiveX controls will not be affected.

Using form templates

Many Visual Basic projects use more than one form. Common forms to include are dialogs where the user can set options, an About box which describes the application and gives copyright details, and a Splash form which shows when the application starts up.

Visual Basic can create forms like this automatically. They are still standard forms, but by using templates the initial design is done for you. There is a double advantage. First, it saves you some work, and second, it gives the forms a standard look and feel which makes your project more professional in appearance.

How to use form templates

There will be different form templates available depending on which version of Visual Basic you have installed.

1 From the Project menu, choose Add Form. A list of templates appears. Choose the first one, Form, for a standard form, or select a template. In this example, the About dialog is chosen.

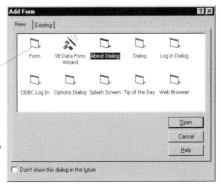

If the templates dialog does not appear, it means that Form Templates have been turned off in the Tools > Options >Environment dialog.

2 Next, the pre-designed form appears. From here, you can select and edit the objects as you want. You can display the form in your application with the code:

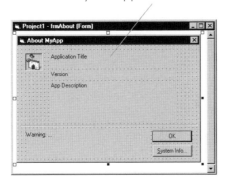

`frmAbout.Show`

or

`frmAbout.Show vbModal`

if you want the user to close the form before continuing.

Using project templates

You never have to use a Project Template. All the options can be selected manually from other Visual Basic dialogs.

Project templates are like the Form Template feature, except that instead of creating a form, the project template sets various options to suit a particular kind of application.

The various ActiveX options are beyond the scope of this book, but one that is interesting is the Application Wizard. This takes you through a series of steps and at the end produces a skeleton application complete with features like a splash screen and an About box.

The problem with the Application Wizard is that most of the real work is still to be done. If you click on one of the toolbar icons or menu options, the chances are that you will just get a message, "... code goes here". For that reason, if you are learning Visual Basic, the Standard EXE is usually the best choice. The Application Wizard is worth a look, though, if only to see an example of how to design menus, toolbars and status bars.

Many wizards let you load and save settings as profiles. This way, you can recall previously used settings to speed your work.

To use the Application Wizard, choose New Project from the File menu. Then choose the Wizard from the project template dialog.

If you see dialog options which you do not yet understand, it is usually best to leave them at the default settings.

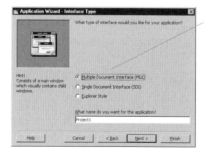

2 Choose from the options in the Wizard dialogs, clicking Next to move on. Finally, click Finish to have Visual Basic create the application.

Creating a stand-alone application

As you learn Visual Basic, you will soon create applications which you want to use without having to run them from within the programming environment. You will also want to make them available to others.

This page explains how to create a stand-alone executable. To distribute programs to others, you need to learn about the Package & Deployment Wizard, explained on pages 183–185.

1 To create a stand-alone executable, load your project and choose Make (YourApp).EXE from the File menu. Enter a name for the executable program, and navigate to the directory where you want to create it.

If you have used custom icon in your application, for example by setting the icon property for a form, you can choose which icon to use for the executable. This will show up in Explorer as the program icon. A range of icons is supplied with Visual Basic.

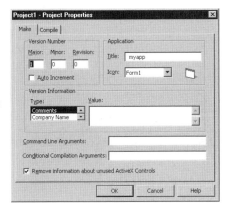

2 If you choose Options, the relevant parts of the Project Properties dialog appear. A handy option is to embed version and copyright information in the executable. On the Compile tab you can choose between p-code and native code. See page 86 for more details.

3 When you are happy with the options, return to the Make EXE dialog and choose OK to create the executable. You can now exit Visual Basic and run this like any other application.

Adding a shortcut to the Start menu

When you have created a stand-alone application, you will want to put it on the Start menu so you can easily find it. Here is how to do it.

When you use the Setup Wizard to distribute Visual Basic programs, you can have your program added automatically to the Start menu. The technique here is handy for installing programs on your own system.

Open Explorer, and navigate to where you stored the stand-alone executable. Select it, and from the Edit menu choose Copy.

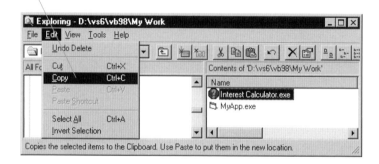

2 Now place the mouse over the Start button on the taskbar, right-click, and choose Explore. The Start menu opens in Explorer view. Navigate to where you want your program to appear, and choose Paste Shortcut from the Edit menu.

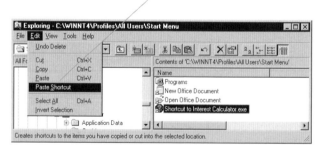

There are other ways to add programs to the Start menu. For instance, you can drag an executable from Explorer onto the Start button. Another technique is to right-click the Taskbar, choose Properties, choose the Start menu programs tab, and click Add.

Creating Databases

Visual Basic is ideal for managing data, since it has a built-in database engine which does all the hard work for you. Data stored by Visual Basic can also be used by other applications like Microsoft Access or Word. This chapter explains how to get started, creating an example database application for a small club. It also shows how to manage database connections, enabling you to add queries and create reports.

Covers

Chapter Five

Introducing databases

A database is simply a collection of information, or data. In a sense, even a list in a word-processor document or spreadsheet is a simple database. Such lists are inflexible and hard to manage once they get beyond a certain size. Visual Basic is able to handle small and large databases easily. You can create forms for searching, updating or reporting on data. You can also use BASIC code to perform calculations or process large numbers of records in one batch.

There are a few words that database programmers use in a special way. It is worth remembering what they mean.

A table

The best way to learn how Visual Basic databases work is to create one. That is what you will be doing, step by step, in this chapter.

A table is a list of information organized into fields or columns. Usually each field has a fixed length.

A table displayed in Microsoft Access

Records or rows

A record is a single row in the list. Tables are sometimes viewed a single record at a time, rather than as a list in a grid.

A database

A database is a collection of tables which are related in some way. For example, you might have a table of customers and another table of orders. Some databases only consist of one table.

Structured Query Language (SQL)

If you spend much time working with Visual Basic databases, you will have come across references to SQL. This is a language used to query and update data. You do not need to learn this to get started, but it is used a lot in advanced database programming, and not only by Visual Basic.

Using Visual Data Manager

Visual Data Manager is an Add-in. You will find it on the Add-in menu. It is a utility for creating and managing databases, written in Visual Basic. You can think of it as a simplified version of Microsoft Access. It is used here for the first step in database work, designing and creating the file that will hold the data.

Visual Data Manager comes with the Professional and Enterprise versions of Visual Basic. If you have the Standard version, you cannot create databases, only use existing ones. An alternative is to use Access to create the database.

Using Visual Data Manager, you will be creating a database to manage a sports club. You can easily adapt it to store general addresses, a book collection, or any other kind of data.

1   Use Windows Explorer to create a directory for your databases. The name used in this example is C:\MYDATA.

2   From the Add-in menu, run the Visual Data Manager. From its File menu, choose New>Microsoft Access>Version 7.0 MDB. In the File Selection dialog that appears, navigate to C:\MYDATA and type the name SPORTS.MDB.

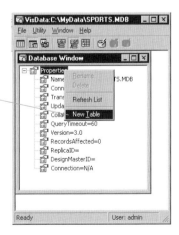

If you already have a database you want to work with, turn to page 99, "Building a data form".

3   In the Database window that appears, right-click over the word Properties. A pop-up menu appears. Choose New Table. Now turn to the next page to continue designing your database.

Designing a table

Now it is time to define the structure of the table. This important step determines what kind of information can be stored.

1 When you choose New Table, the Table Structure dialog opens. In the Name box at top-left, type Members.

2 Next, click Add field. For now, only edit four of the boxes. Leave the others at the default.
Under Name put LastName.
Under Type choose Text.
Under Size enter 30.
Click Required so it is checked.

3 When you click OK, the field is added to the list. The Add Field dialog stays open, however, so you can add more fields, until you finally click Close. Here is the full list of fields:

Name	Type	Size	Required
LastName	Text	30	Checked
FirstName	Text	30	Not Checked
Address1	Text	50	Not Checked
Address2	Text	50	Not Checked
Town	Text	50	Not Checked
State	Text	50	Not Checked
Zip	Text	15	Not Checked
Telephone	Text	30	Not Checked
Notes	Memo	n/a	Not Checked
ID	Long	4	Checked*

For the ID field, do not forget to check AutoIncField.

*Also check AutoIncrField

Now see the next page to continue the table design.

4 Next, click Add
Index to create
indexes for the
new table.
Indexes speed up
sorting and
searching of the
data. There are
two to add:

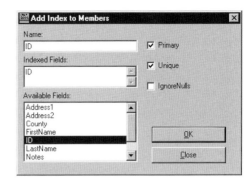

*There is
another setting,
called
IgnoreNulls,
which you can
leave at the default
(unchecked).*

Name	Indexed Fields	Primary	Unique
ID	ID	Checked	Checked
LastName	LastName	Not checked	Not checked

Finally, click Close to close the Add Index dialog.

5 Here is how
the Table
Structure
dialog looks
when you
have finished.
Now click
"Build the
Table" to
actually create
the table.

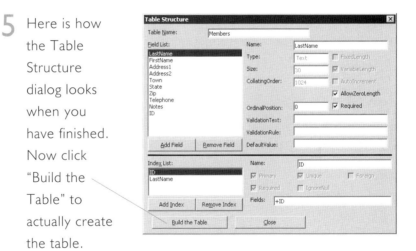

*You should not
remove fields
once data has
been added.
That would
delete all the data in that
field.*

If you have made any mistakes, there are two ways to correct
them. One is by highlighting the field, which lets you edit
some properties like the Required setting. Some settings,
like Size, can only be changed by removing the field and
adding a new one.

Adding data

The database you have created is empty. Here is how to use Visual Data Manager to add or edit data.

1   Run Visual Data Manager. On the toolbar make sure the icons for Table type Recordset and Use Data Control are depressed.

You can also open a table for editing by double-clicking its name.

2   Use File>Open to open the SPORTS.MDB database. Right-click the name of the Members table and choose Open from the pop-up menu.

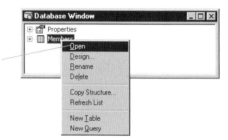

3   Because the table is empty, the text at the bottom of the form which appears says "Add record". Enter some example data in the fields. Note you do not need to enter an ID number. Then click Update. A dialog appears, confirming this. Click Yes to save the new record.

You can add further records if you like, by clicking Add, entering the details, and then clicking Update.

4   Visual Basic adds an ID Number automatically. Now that you have added a record, the text at the bottom says 1/1.

More about database tables

Using the Visual Data Manager introduces some key features of database tables.

Field type

Fields in a database table have a data type, similar to those used by Visual Basic for variables. You need to choose field types appropriate for the data to be stored. Some of the most important are:

Text – for strings of characters like names, addresses and telephone numbers. You can set the maximum number of characters up to 255.

These data types apply to tables in MDB format, the format used by Microsoft Access and by Visual Basic. You can also use other kinds of data table with Visual Basic, such as dBase format. dBase has different data types. This book only covers MDB databases.

Integer and Long – for whole numbers. The Integer type is smaller, and can only hold numbers up to 32,767. Long number fields can be set to AutoIncrement, which means each record will automatically be assigned the next available number.

Memo – for strings of up to 65,535 characters. You cannot specify the length.

Boolean – for true or false values.

Single and Double – for floating-point numbers. The Double can hold larger numbers and with greater precision.

Currency – for money values

Date/Time – for date and time values.

Other field properties

Two of the fields, LastName and ID, were set as Required. That means all records in the table must have some entry for that field.

Primary Key

The term "Primary Key" is database jargon for an indexed field which uniquely identifies each record.

The ID field was indexed as Primary and Unique. It is also marked to AutoIncrement. This combination means that every record can be reliably identified by its ID field. This is an essential feature of well-designed data tables.

Introducing the Data Control

The easiest way to display data on a Visual Basic form is to use an object called the Data Control. The Data Control represents a database table or query (see below). When you are designing your form, you set the properties of the data control to tell it which database to use, and which table or query to extract from the database.

Visual Basic 6.0 actually has two data controls, or three in the Enterprise version. They are not interchangeable, so make sure you use the right one.

Next, you build up your form by placing other controls such as text boxes or list boxes on it. These will display fields from the database, and are called bound controls. For example, a text box has a DataSource property which you can set to link it to the Data Control, and a DataField property which indicates which field to display. When you run the form, the requested data appears.

The Data Control has built-in buttons for operations like moving forward or back through the data. As it does so, the fields showing in bound controls automatically update, which is why they are called "bound".

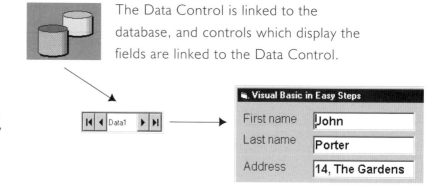

The Data Control is linked to the database, and controls which display the fields are linked to the Data Control.

Turn to the next page to see the Data Control at work.

What is a query?

The term "query" means the set of data that results from applying search conditions. For example, you could ask to see all records with a last name of "Smith". You can set the data control to represent a query rather than a table. You can also create queries that draw data from several tables, so queries are more flexible.

Building a data form

This example uses the club database created earlier in this chapter.

This is the Data Control icon in the toolbox.

1 Start a new form and place on it a Data Control, two text boxes and a label. Set the label's caption to "Name", and the Data Control's caption to "Members".

Visual Basic's Data Form Wizard will create a data form automatically. It is worth building one from scratch, though, to learn how it all fits together.

2 Select the Data Control and view its properties. Click on the three dots to the right of the DatabaseName property, and navigate to SPORTS.MDB to link it to the Sports database.

3 Next to the RecordSource property, again for the Data Control, is a drop-down arrow. Click here and choose Members.

4 Now select each text box, and set the DataSource property to Data1. Then change the DataField property to FirstName and LastName respectively. When you run the form, this field data appears in the text boxes.

Improving the data form

The data form you have created has some basic features. You can move back and forth through the Members table, with the current name displayed.

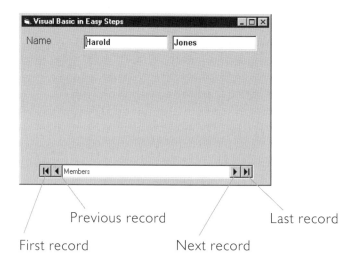

Previous record

Last record

First record

Next record

There are a number of features that need to be added. You need to be able to see more fields, add and delete records, and search for a particular record.

Adding fields

To save time, you can select several text boxes and set the DataSource property once for all of them.

To add fields, place further labels and text boxes for the fields you want. Set the DataSource to link to the Data Control, and the FieldName properties to the fields required.

There is no need to display the ID field on the form, as in most circumstances this is not meaningful for the user.

By adding further bound text boxes, all the fields from the Members table can be displayed. The Notes field has its Multiline property set to True, and ScrollBars to Vertical, to allow long notes to be displayed.

Adding records

So far, you have created a data form without writing any code. To add and delete records, a small amount of Basic is required. Most of your code will be calling methods of the Data Control's RecordSet property. This property is an object which represents the current set of records. In the example, this is equivalent to the whole Members table, but in other circumstances it might be a query result rather than a complete table.

How to Add a record

If you prefer not to use buttons on a form, you could use a menu instead.

1 You will need to make room for some buttons at the bottom of the form. Place one and give it the name cbAdd and the Caption "Add". Then add this code to its Click event:

```
Data1.Recordset.AddNew
```

For a more consistent look, try setting the Data Control's Visible property to False. Add your own buttons for moving back and forth, calling the methods of the invisible Data Control in your code.

2 When you run the form, click Add to create a new, blank record. Fill in the data. As soon as you click the data control to move to another record, the data is saved.

If you try to add a record with no LastName, Visual Basic pops up a warning. This is because LastName was set as a required field when the table was designed.

Deleting records

The technique for deleting a record is very similar to that for adding a new one, although there are a couple of other issues to consider. One is confirmation. You cannot recover a record once it is deleted, so it makes sense to ask the user to confirm the deletion.

The other issue is less obvious. When you call a Recordset's Delete method, the record is deleted but the deleted record still shows up in the field values. It is only when you move off the record, by going back or forward in the recordset, that the record really disappears. Therefore, we need to add code to move away from the record after deleting it.

If you leave a deleted record showing, Visual Basic will very likely produce this error.

Code to delete a record

Here is the code for a Delete button:

Note the use of With, which means all the dotted properties or methods within the block apply to the Data1.Recordset object.

```
With Data1.Recordset
If MsgBox("Really delete " + .Fields("LastName") + _
   "?", vbYesNo) = vbYes Then
      .Delete ' Deletes the record
   .MoveNext ' Moves to the next record
   If .EOF Then .MoveLast ' Move to the last record
End If
End With
```

Getting the value of a field

In the above code, the value of the LastName field is included in the confirmation dialog. Note the expression used:

```
Data1.RecordSet.Fields("LastName").
```

See the next page for why this code can cause an error.

A dialog to confirm deletion

Preventing Data Control errors

Although building data forms with the Data Control is quick, you need to watch for some subtle errors. The problem is that certain actions are not always valid. For example, if the recordset is empty, the methods for moving backwards or forwards produce an error. If the recordset is beyond the last record, attempting to move forward raises an error. Often you can avoid these by checking for certain conditions in code. For instance:

If you move beyond the last record in a recordset, the EOF property (End Of File) is set to True and there is no current record. The equivalent is true for the first record and BOF (Beginning Of File).

```
If Dat1.Recordset.EOF then
Data1.Recordset.MoveLast
End If
```

When a recordset is empty, both EOF and BOF are true. So you can check for it like this:

```
If not (Data1.RecordSet.EOF and _
    Data1.RecordSet.BOF) then
Data1.RecordSet.MoveFirst
End If
```

More about No Current Record

Visual Basic database applications are most vulnerable to errors when there is no current record. The main reasons are if EOF or BOF is true, or if the Delete method has just been used, or if AddNew has been called but the database has not yet been updated by moving the recordset to a different record. This last problem is the most difficult. There are three ways to solve it:

You need to take even more care if you are sharing data with others on a network. Networked databases are beyond the scope of this book, but covered in the Visual Basic on-line help.

1.   You can disable actions that cause an error. For example, when you click the Add button to call AddNew, you could introduce code to disable the Delete button, by setting its Enabled property False.

2.   You can avoid this state by calling the Update method immediately after AddNew. In this case, you would need to put a dummy value like "NewName" in the required LastName field, or the update fails.

3.   You can write code to handle the error gracefully. See pages 160–161 for how to handle errors.

Viewing records in order

The data form you have created for the Sports club does not seem to show records in any particular order. In fact, they are displayed in the order they were created, which is not usually convenient. You probably want to view the club members ordered by the LastName field. Here are two ways to do it.

1. Select the Data Control and ensure that its RecordsetType property is set to Table.

You can only set the Index of a recordset if it is of Table type.

2. Double-click the form to open its event code. Find the Activate event in the right-hand drop-down list Add this line of code:

```
Data1.Recordset.Index = "LastName"
```

A better technique

The following technique seems a little more complex but is a better, more flexible approach.

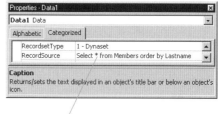

1. Make sure you delete the code added in step 2 above. Then select the Data Control and ensure that its RecordsetType property is set to Dynaset. Now click in the RecordSource property and type:

```
Select * from Members Order By LastName
```

Although you can use Order By on fields which are not indexed, this will result in poor performance.

What you have done is to write a simple SQL query which asks for all the records in the Members table in LastName order. This is totally flexible, and will even work if there is no LastName index.

Explaining Dynasets and Tables

If you followed through the example on the previous page, you may have wondered what a Dynaset was. In Visual Basic, there are three kinds of RecordSet. A RecordSet is the set of records represented by a Data Control.

If you do advanced work with Visual Basic databases, you will find that you can also create RecordSets without using the Data Control.

Table type

A Table RecordSet is simply a complete database table. The advantage of this type is that they are easy to set up, and some operations are very fast. You can set the Index property of a Table, which you cannot do with other types of RecordSet. That means you can also use the Seek method, which is the fastest way to search for a record.

Table types are inflexible and have a major disadvantage. If the database is large, a complete Table represents an unmanageable number of records. This is awkward for the user and makes performance poor as well.

Dynaset type

A Dynaset is the most useful general-purpose RecordSet. Dynasets are created by specifying an SQL query as the recordsource. Because SQL is a powerful query language, Dynasets are very flexible. They are called Dynasets (short for Dynamic Sets) because if the data changes while the Dynaset is open, for example on a network, the Dynaset automatically shows the changed data. You can usually update the data in Dynasets.

You can use a Data Control for all three of these RecordSet types.

Snapshot type

A Snapshot is also created with a SQL query, but unlike a Dynaset, the data in a Snapshot is fixed once it is opened. You will not see any changes made afterwards by others, and you cannot update the Snapshot data or add new records.

Snapshots are very efficient if you want read-only access to a small RecordSet. In other cases, Dynasets are usually preferable.

Searching for records

Once a database grows beyond a trivial size, it is vital to have a quick way of finding the record you want. Here is a simple technique for searching the Sports database.

This technique does not work for Table-type RecordSets.

Add a search button to the form. Give a name of "cbSearch" and a caption, "Search". Then double-click to open its Click event.

Note the use of a Bookmark to mark your place in the RecordSet and return to it later.

Enter the following code:

```
Private Sub cbSearch_Click()
Dim searchvar As String
Dim sBookMark As String
searchvar = InputBox("Enter the Lastname to
find")
searchvar = Trim$(searchvar) ' removes surplus
spaces
   If searchvar <> "" Then 'cancel if nothing
entered
   With Data1.Recordset
   sBookMark = .Bookmark
   .FindFirst "Lastname like '" + searchvar + "*'"
     If .NoMatch Then ' record not found
     MsgBox "No matching record"
     .Bookmark = sBookMark
     End If
   End With
   End If
End Sub
```

See the next page for a more detailed explanation of FindFirst.

Searches in Visual Basic are not case-sensitive.

Run the form and click Search. You will be asked to enter a last name. Type a name that exists, click OK, and the record appears. If it is not found, the record does not change.

The most common type of RecordSet used in Visual Basic is a Dynaset, and the easiest way to search one is with the FindFirst method. The parameter for FindFirst looks odd at first. It is a single string but needs to be formatted correctly. A typical FindFirst parameter is like this:

If you know SQL, it will help to know that the FindFirst parameter is the WHERE clause of an SQL query.

```
FindFirst "LastName = 'Jones' "
```

Note that the name being sought is surrounded by single quote characters.

Usually, you want the user to be able to enter a search value at runtime. Therefore, you need to store the user's search value in a variable, and use it to build up a string of the kind FindFirst needs to see. The secret is to put single quotes within double quotes like this:

If you need to search a table-type RecordSet, use the Seek method.

```
FindFirst "LastName = '" + sSearchvar + "'"
```

Using LIKE

A great feature of FindFirst is that you can use LIKE in place of "=". Then you can use wildcards in the search string. The user can enter "Jon" and still find "Jones". You do this by adding a "*" to the end of the word, still within the single quotes:

```
FindFirst "LastName LIKE '" + sSearchvar + "*'"
```

Using AND

FindFirst is actually a powerful query command. You can build up complex conditions using operators such as: AND, OR, AND NOT. For clarity, a good idea is to surround each part of the query with brackets:

```
FindFirst "(Lastname = 'Jones') AND (FirstName = 'Jane')"
```

After all the Find... methods, you can check NoMatch to see if the search succeeded.

FindNext, FindPrevious, FindLast

These commands are just like FindFirst, except that as their names imply, they work in different directions. FindNext looks for the next occurrence after the current record.

Showing records in a grid

Another popular way to view records is in a grid. The advantage of grids is that you can see more than one record at a time. With Visual Basic's bound grid control, it is easy to create grid views of your data.

How to show records in a grid

Creating a grid-based data form is the quickest way to have a working Visual Basic database application.

1 Right-click the Toolbox, choose Components, and make sure Microsoft Data Grid Control is checked.

2 This example is based on the previous data form, but with the labels and text boxes deleted. Before you do so, you might like to right-click the form in the Project Explorer and Save As a different name, say Gridform.frm. Then you will not lose your work. Then, delete the labels and text boxes, and place a DBGrid on the form. Set its DataSource to the Data Control. Set its AllowAddNew property to True.

You can combine a data-bound grid with other bound controls. For example, place a text box on the form bound to the Notes field. As you click on records in the grid, the Notes field updates automatically.

3 Run the application, and all your records show in a scrolling grid. Click in the bottom row of the grid to add a record. The Add and Delete buttons also work.

Copying a record to the Clipboard

A handy technique if you have a database of addresses is to be able to copy an address to the Windows Clipboard. Then you can easily paste it into a document, for example a letter.

The Clipboard Object

This example works just the same whether your data form has a grid or record view.

Visual Basic has an invisible Clipboard object. It has methods for setting or retrieving its contents. In this example, all you need is the Clear method, which empties the clipboard, and the SetText method, which adds a string to the clipboard.

Adding a Clipboard button

1 Add a button named "cbClip" to the data form, and give it the caption "Clipboard".

For the best result, you can improve this code by testing whether fields are empty before adding them to the sAddress string. That avoids blank lines when you paste the address into a document.

2 Double-click the button to open its Click event, and enter the following code:

```
Private Sub cbClip_Click()
Dim cr As String
Dim sAddress As String
cr = Chr(13) & Chr(10) ' this creates a new line
character
    With Data1.Recordset
    sAddress = .Fields("FirstName") + " "
    sAddress = sAddress + .Fields("LastName") + cr
    sAddress = sAddress + .Fields("Address1") + cr
    ' add other fields here as needed
    End With
Clipboard.Clear
Clipboard.SetText (sAddress)
MsgBox "The address is on the clipboard"
End Sub
```

Introducing the Data Environment

The data control is useful, but less convenient when you have several forms in your application, all of which need to display data. Visual Basic has a Data Environment which is a component for managing database connections. Both forms and reports can then link to the Data Environment to show and update data.

For a simple application you will not need to use the Data Environment, unless you want to create reports. There is even a way to create reports without it, by using Crystal Reports instead. Crystal Reports is not installed by default, but is an extra on the Visual Basic CD.

The Data Environment uses a different kind of database connection than the examples earlier in this chapter. This kind of connection is called OLE DB or ADO (Activex Data Objects). You can still use the sports club database you have created, but the software that reads the data is different.

One advantage of the Data Environment is that it lets you use Visual Basic's built-in report designer.

Adding a Data Environment to a project

1   Start a new project and then choose Add Data Environment from the Project menu.

2   A Data Environment now appears in the Project Manager. Double-click it to open the Data Environment window.

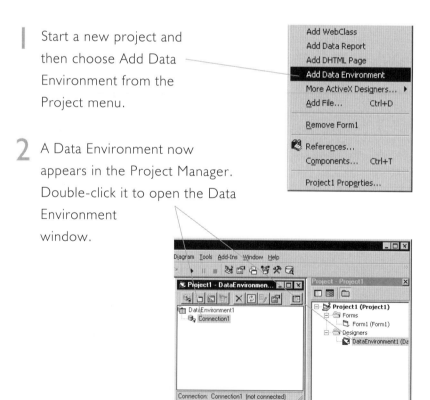

Connecting to data

A Data Environment can manage several different database connections. Here is how to link it to the example Sports database:

 You can rename the connection to something like SportsData, to clarify what the connection is for.

1 In the Data Environment window, right-click Connection1 and choose Properties.

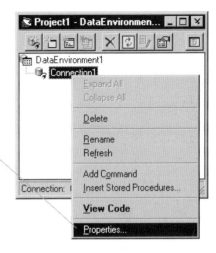

2 From the Provider tab, choose Microsoft Jet OLE DB Provider.

 The exact list of OLE DB providers depends on what your installation choices were and which version of Visual Basic you have.

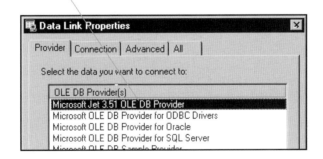

3 Click the Connection tab and then the dotted button by "Select or enter a database name". Navigate to the SPORTS.MDB database and click OK. Finally, click Test Connection to ensure a valid link. You will see a message confirming success.

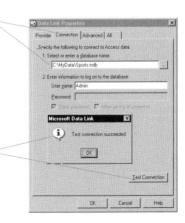

Adding a query

Adding a connection to a Data Environment is only the first stage. To obtain data, it is necessary to add a query. These are known as Commands because they are statements written in SQL (Structured Query Language). Here is how to get a list of Sports Club members:

You need to connect to a database (see previous page) before adding a command.

1 In the Data Environment, right click a connection and choose Add Command.

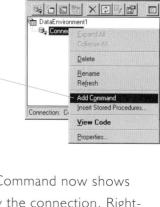

You will see many other options in the Data Environment dialogs. For now, you can safely leave these at the default values.

2 The Command now shows below the connection. Right-click and choose Properties to display the dialog below.

3 Make sure the General tab of the dialog is displayed and click the option for SQL Statement. Then type this statement in the box underneath:

```
SELECT Members.* FROM Members ORDER BY LastName
```

The SQL Builder button opens a visual query designer that saves having to know SQL. With simple queries though, it is easier just to type them in.

4 Click OK to close the dialog.

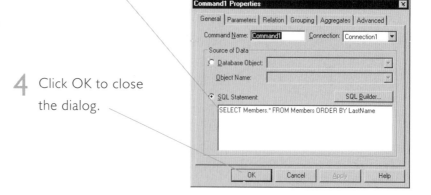

Creating a report

One essential element of most database projects is a report facility. For example, a sports club might want to print out a member list. Visual Basic comes with an integrated report designer. Here is an example of how to create a telephone list, using the Data Environment and connection described in the previous few pages.

1   To add a report to a project, choose Add Data Report from the Project menu.

If the drop-down list for the DataSource does not show the Data Environment then you need to follow the steps on the preceding pages to add it to the project and connect it to data.

2   Display the properties for the Data Report and drop-down the DataSource property. Choose DataEnvironment1. Next, drop-down the DataMember property and choose Command1.

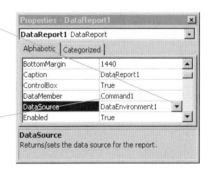

3   Display the report designer and Data Environment side by side. Click the + sign on Command1. It becomes a – sign, expanding to show the list of fields. Next, click on the LastName field, hold down the mouse

You have to choose the DataSource before you can choose the DataMember.

button, and drag it to the Detail panel in the report. Do the same for FirstName and Telephone. Don't worry if it looks untidy at first: you can improve the layout later.

Laying out a report

Once the database connection has been made, designing a report is similar to designing a form. Reports have their own toolbox panel with controls that you can select and drag onto the report surface. You can also select these controls, and display and amend their properties.

You need to connect to a database (see previous page) before adding a command.

The Report toolbox panel   The Report designer   Properties for a text box

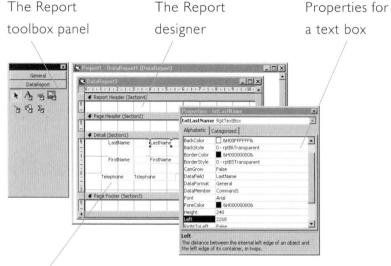

It is not essential to drag fields from the Data Environment to create a report. You can also place text boxes on a form and set their DataMember and DataField properties to bind them to a field.

1   To improve the telephone list, select the label control for each field and press Delete to remove it, leaving just the text box on its right.

2   Then arrange the three text boxes in a line. Drag the bar below the detail panel up, to leave just enough room for the line of text boxes.

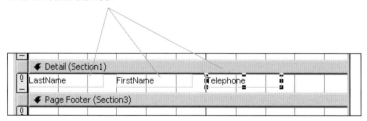

3 Add a label to the Report Header and type a heading. Change its font to a large, bold style.

For really good-looking reports, you can also add lines and graphics.

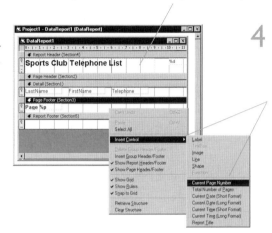

4 Right-click in a section area and choose Insert Control to display a list of special labels such as date and page number controls. Put the date in the header and the page number in the footer.

Advanced users can create groups and sub-groups in reports, and also insert formulas for calculating fields and summaries.

5 When you are happy with the report, place a button on a form and add the code shown to its click event. This will display the report.

HTML is the format used by the Web, so export in HTML if you want to use your report on a web site or intranet.

6 Run the application and click Show to test the report. The runtime window has print and zoom buttons. There is also an Export button which lets you save in text or HTML format.

The next step with databases

Visual Basic is a little harder to use than stand-alone database applications like Microsoft Access, but has several advantages. One is that many of Visual Basic's general development features are also useful in database projects. Another advantage is that if you want to distribute a completed database application, it is easier to do so with Visual Basic. The lack of interactive features in Visual Basic can actually be an advantage, if you want a database application which limits the user's actions to ones that you know are safe for the data.

Working with Access

Visual Basic and Microsoft Access make excellent partners. You can use Access to create databases, set up validation rules, and do interactive editing, while using Visual Basic to develop a packaged application. You can also pass code between the two, since Access also uses Visual Basic for database programming.

Getting relational

More advanced databases use several linked tables. For example, a company might use separate tables for customers, orders and products. A database for a CD collection might have tables for CDs, Tracks and Artists. These relational databases give more power and flexibility, but are substantially harder to manage than single-table databases like the Sports Club example.

ODBC stands for Open Database Connectivity. To connect to a particular database, you need a suitable ODBC driver. Some are supplied with Visual Basic's Enterprise edition.

Going Client-Server

Visual Basic supports a technology called ODBC, as well OLE DB as used for the example report. These let you connect not only to Access MDB databases, but also to server database systems like SQL Server, Oracle or DB2. This is the most complex type of database programming, but is necessary for good performance on large networks, say of 10 or more users.

Visual Basic can keep pace with all your database needs, from small one-user applications to heavyweight client-server systems.

Visual Basic in Office

One of the most exciting features of Visual Basic is that it comes, in a slightly different form, as part of Microsoft Office. Every Office user can take advantage of it.

This chapter tells you how to use Visual Basic in Office, including recording macros and creating forms and dialogs.

It also explains how you can control Office applications from Visual Basic, using Word and Excel as tools in your own projects.

Chapter Six

Covers

About Visual Basic for Applications

Visual Basic for Applications, or VBA, is Microsoft's name for the programming language built in to Office, and available to other vendors to integrate into their applications as well. To explain the difference between VBA and the stand-alone version of Visual Basic, you need to distinguish between two elements:

1.   The core Visual Basic language.

2.   Objects like buttons, list boxes and ActiveX controls which are made available for programming.

The core language is the same wherever Visual Basic is used, whether it is stand-alone or in VBA; it is the set of available objects which changes. Each VBA-enabled application has its own set of objects which you can use in your code. For example, Word has Document and Paragraph objects. Once you have learned to program these objects, there are few limits to what you can do with your VBA code.

There is another significant point. If you have Office installed, then all those Office objects are available to all versions of Visual Basic. So you can program Word from Excel, or from the stand-alone version of Visual Basic.

VBA is part of Excel, Word, Access, PowerPoint, and FrontPage from version 2000. Outlook uses another version of Visual Basic called VB Script, which is less powerful.

Other differences

VBA has a form editor and debugger much like the one in the stand-alone version, but with a more limited set of features. You cannot compile stand-alone .EXE files from VBA, and there is no native code compiler. There is no data control either, although you can still access databases through pure VBA code.

VBA has a great feature of its own: you can get started by recording macros, which means Office is writing the code for you.

The VBA programming tool

Visual Basic for Applications has its own visual programming environment. This is the same in all the Office applications.

Opening VBA from an Office application

To open Visual Basic for Applications, choose Tools>Macro>Visual Basic Editor.

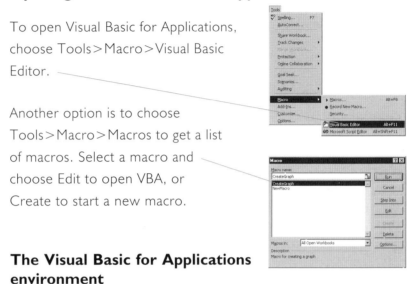

Another option is to choose Tools>Macro>Macros to get a list of macros. Select a macro and choose Edit to open VBA, or Create to start a new macro.

Keyboard shortcuts are usually the same between Visual Basic and Visual Basic for Applications. For example, press F5 to run.

The Visual Basic for Applications environment

The programming environment runs as if it were a separate application. It is very similar to the stand-alone Visual Basic.

Run button   Code editor   Properties window

Project Explorer

Toolbox

Form designer

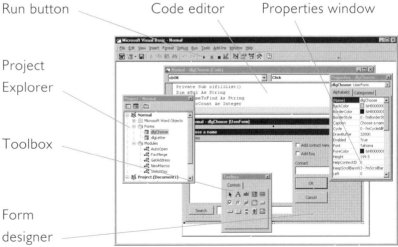

Recording a macro in Excel

1. Start Excel and ensure that a new, empty workbook is loaded. Then choose Tools>Macro>Record New Macro.

Macros write Visual Basic code for you, so recording a macro is a good way to get started with VBA.

2. In the dialog that appears, type a name for the macro, e.g. OpenMacro. Ensure that "This Workbook" is chosen under "Store macro in". Then click OK.

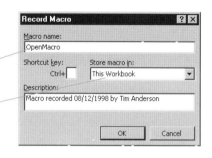

3. Note the small macro-recording window which appears. While you see this window, your actions are being recorded. Now choose Excel's File>Open menu option and open a workbook of your choice. When the workbook opens, click the Stop Recording button.

When you record a macro, you should pay attention to where it is stored. The macro is only available if the workbook in which it is stored is currently loaded. You can also store macros in a template, to make them available for all workbooks based on that template.

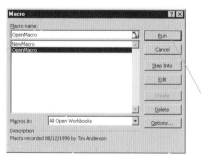

4. You can easily test the macro. Close the workbook which you have just opened. Go to the Tools>Macro>Macros menu option, then select OpenMacro and click Run. The workbook opens again.

Understanding the macro

1 To see the macro you have created, make sure the workbook containing the macro is open. Then choose Tools>Macro>Macros to open the macro list. Select the macro and click Edit.

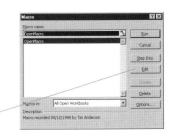

To learn the names of Excel's objects, use the on-line help for Visual Basic in Excel.

2 Visual Basic now opens with your OpenMacro visible in a window. It is at most two lines of code:

```
ChDir "C:\mydata"
```

changes directory to where your workbook is stored, while

```
Workbooks.Open FileName:="C:\mydata\myfile.xls"
```

actually opens the file. "Workbooks" is a collection of Excel objects representing all the open workbooks in Excel. "Open" is a method of Workbooks which tells Excel to open the specified workbook. "FileName" is a named parameter, which means you can assign a value to it using the ":=" operator. The assigned value is the actual file name including the full path.

Visual Basic Help is not installed by default. If you have Office 97 or earlier, you have to run Setup and choose it as an option. In Office 2000, Windows will normally prompt you to install it when you try to use it.

3 You can enhance the macro by editing the code or adding new instructions. For example, adding the following line would make Excel insert today's date in the first cell:

```
ActiveSheet.Cells(1, 1).Value = Str$(Now)
```

You could also easily amend the code to open a different workbook. The combination of recorded code with manual editing is a powerful one.

Three ways to run a macro

When you have created a macro, there are several ways to run it. You have already seen how you can use the Tools>Macro>Macros option. Here are three more:

1. Use a keyboard shortcut

Although this topic refers to Excel, the same or very similar techniques work in the other Office applications.

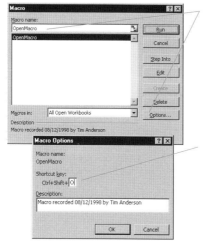

Open the macro list and click Options.

Enter a letter in the Shortcut Key box. Click OK, and then close the macro list. In future, pressing CTRL>Shift>O (or whatever key you chose) will run the macro.

You can also use the Forms toolbar to put a button on a worksheet. This works only in Excel. Form buttons are less flexible, but run more quickly.

2. Use a button on a worksheet

You can place a button on a worksheet itself.

From Excel's View menu choose Toolbars. Ensure that Control Toolbox is checked.

2 Click the button on the Control Toolbox; click and drag it onto the worksheet.

Use this button to exit design mode on an Excel worksheet.

3 Right-click the button, and choose View code to open the Click event. Type the line: `Call OpenMacro` [or your macro name]. Close the code window and exit Design mode. The button will now call your macro.

3. Use a menu option

You can give your macro its own menu option, as follows:

1 From Excel's Tools menu choose Customize. Click the Commands tab and then the Macros item in the scrolling list on the left.

 If you have several custom macros, you might want to create a new toolbar or top-level menu for them. See Excel's on-line help for more details on how to customize menus and toolbars.

2 Now click on the Custom menu item here and hold down the left mouse button.

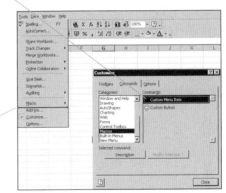

3 Drag the menu item to the Tools menu so it drops down, and then drag down, watching the solid black line which appears. The new menu will be inserted at the position of this line, when you release the left mouse button.

4 Now right-click the mouse over the new menu item. In the Name box type the text for the menu item. Then click Assign Macro and choose your macro. Finally, close the Customize dialog.

Macros that run automatically

You can set macros that run automatically when a document is opened or in response to other events. Here is an example.

Running a macro when an Excel workbook opens

Word documents have an Open event as well.

1 Open a workbook in Excel or start a new one. Open the Visual Basic editor. From the View menu, choose Project Explorer, if it is not already showing. Look for the entry for ThisWorkbook, right-click on it and choose View Code.

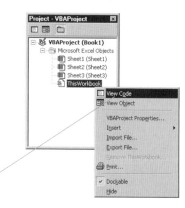

Note the many other events for which you can write code.

2 From the left-hand drop-down list, choose Workbook. In the right-hand list, ensure Open is showing. Then enter some code, for example a MsgBox greeting.

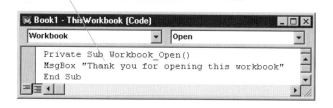

```
Private Sub Workbook_Open()
MsgBox "Thank you for opening this workbook"
End Sub
```

When you open a document which contains macros, you may see a warning dialog. This is for security. If you created the workbook and macros yourself, this will not be a concern.

3 Close the Visual Basic editor and save the workbook. Then open it again. The code runs and the greeting appears. More useful examples could automatically enter the date and time, or set the initial values of global variables.

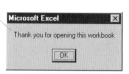

More about the Project Explorer

The Visual Basic for Applications Project Explorer tells you where your code and forms are stored and lets you open them for editing. In Office, Visual Basic code and forms are stored in documents or templates. Therefore, you can think of each document as a VBA project. When you save the document or template, you also save the Visual Basic elements that are stored there.

The best way to learn how the Project Explorer works is to try it out.

The Project Explorer in Excel

Click here to open the code for the selected object

Click here to view the selected object

Click here to see the Project in folder view.

Double-click or click View Code for a sheet or workbook, to write code in response to events like Open or Change.

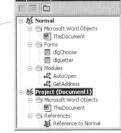

Each document open in Excel is also a project.

Modules contain code such as your own functions and procedures, or global variables.

References in VBA work the same way as in stand-alone Visual Basic.

The Project Explorer in Word

Word's Project Explorer is similar to that of Excel. However, there are differences, like the presence of the Normal template, and the way references are listed.

Code and forms in the Normal template are available to any document.

Using VBA to write values into cells

When you use Visual Basic in Excel, you will often want to write values into cells. Here is a simple procedure that puts some values and a formula into a worksheet.

Named ranges are a useful way of identifying cells in VBA code.

For example, if you have a range called "TotalVal", you can refer to Range("TotalVal") in your code.

Start a new workbook and open the Visual Basic editor. Choose Project Explorer from the View menu if it is not already open. Right-click the project for the current workbook and choose Insert > Module. This now appears as Module1.

The code editor will open automatically. You will be creating a new procedure. You could use the Procedure option from the Insert menu, but it is easier just to click in the code editor and type:

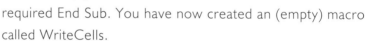

```
Sub WriteCells
```

When you press Enter, VBA automatically puts in the required End Sub. You have now created an (empty) macro called WriteCells.

Here is the code:

```
With ActiveSheet
.Cells(1, 1).Value = "Jan-Mar"
.Cells(1, 2).Value = 123
.Cells(2, 1).Value = "Apr-Jun"
.Cells(2, 2).Value = 456
.Cells(4, 1).Value = "Total"
.Cells(4, 2).Value = "=SUM(B1..B2)"
End With
```

When you enter a formula, use the "+" or "=" operator to tell Excel it is not plain text.

When you run the macro, the values automatically appear in the worksheet.

	A	B
1	Jan-Mar	123
2	Apr-Jun	456
3		
4	Total	579

Entering text from a Word macro

One thing you will soon need to do when working with Word is to insert text into a document. Here is a simple example.

The use of bookmarks in Word is similar to the use of named ranges in Excel. Both are valuable for work with Visual Basic.

1. Create a Word document and put a bookmark in the text, using the Bookmark option from the Insert menu. Name the bookmark, for example, "MyBookmark".

2. Open the Visual Basic editor and ensure the Project Explorer is visible (you can select it from the View menu). Right-click the project for your document and choose Insert Module.

Use the Collapse method to deselect a block of selected text.

Click in the code window and type:

```
Sub WriteText
```

Visual Basic automatically adds the required End Sub. Now type the following code:

```
With ActiveDocument
If .Bookmarks.Exists("MyBookmark") Then
.Bookmarks("MyBookMark").Select
End If

Selection.InsertAfter ("This text was entered from a macro")
Selection.Collapse (wdCollapseEnd)
```

You can run the macro either from within the Visual Basic editor, or from the Word document itself, using the Tools> Macros option.

3. Run the macro and check the Word document. Text has been automatically entered.

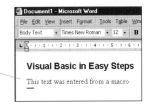

Creating a dialog in Word

Visual Basic earns its "Visual" title when you use it to create applications which include forms and dialogs. Although the example on this page is a simple one, there are few limits to what you can do with a VBA form. You can even use ActiveX controls in a form, which makes possible things like charts, multimedia and animations.

Creating and using a dialog

The aim of this project is to build a macro that will start a new document based on one of two templates.

If you want to use a macro regularly, it is best to store it in Normal.dot rather than in a document. For experiments though, a document is better.

1   Start a new document in Word, then open Visual Basic. View the Project Explorer, right-click the project associated with the new document, and choose Insert>User Form. A blank form will open, and the toolbox will appear.

2   Design the form as you would in stand-alone Visual Basic. It uses two option buttons and two command buttons, with captions as shown. Set the value property of the top option button to True. Set the Default property of the OK button to True, and the Cancel property of the Cancel button to True.

The Default and Cancel properties determine how the dialog works if the user presses Enter or Escape.

3   Double-click the form to open its code. In the right drop-down list, choose General. The left drop-down should read Declarations. Then click in the editor and type:

`Public DocOption as Integer`

This variable will be used to store the user's choice from the dialog.

An even better approach is to use property procedures to get and set the public result of the dialog box.

4 Double-click the OK button to open its Click event. Type the following code:

```
If OptionButton1.Value = True Then
UserForm1.DocOption = 1
ElseIf OptionButton2.Value = True Then
UserForm1.DocOption = 2
Else
UserForm1.DocOption = 0
End If
Me.Hide
```

Double-click the Cancel button and enter this one line:

```
Me.Hide
```

5 Next, insert a module into the project, or open it if it already exists. Open it in the code editor and type:

```
Sub DocStart()
UserForm1.DocOption = 0
UserForm1.Show
Select Case UserForm1.DocOption
Case 1 ' General doc
Documents.Add ' will use Normal.DOT
Case 2 ' Letter doc
Documents.Add Template:="C:\Program _
  Files\Microsoft Office\Templates\Letters & _
  Faxes\Professional Letter.dot"
End Select
End Sub
```

You should amend this line for the correct path and file name for your system. On Windows NT the templates are usually stored in your user's Profile directory.

6 Close Visual Basic and return to Word. Then run the DocStart macro. It starts a new document with the chosen template.

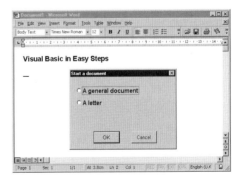

Reading a database from Word

If the DAO Object Library does not appear in References, run the Office setup and install Microsoft Query. The DAO library will be installed with it. Older versions of Office will have an earlier version of DAO.

One of the most useful parts of VBA is the ability to read data stored in databases. This example uses the SPORTS.MDB data file created in Chapter Five. To prepare it, first open a Word document and insert a bookmark called MyBookmark. Next, open the Visual Basic editor and then the Tools > References dialog and check the DAO 3.5 Object Library. Create a new module and type the following macro:

```
Sub ReadSports()
Dim db As database
Dim rs As recordset
Set db = DAO.OpenDatabase("C:\MYDATA\SPORTS.MDB")
Set rs = db.OpenRecordset("SELECT * FROM MEMBERS ORDER BY
LASTNAME")
If Not (rs.BOF And rs.EOF) Then
 rs.MoveFirst
  ActiveDocument.Bookmarks("MyBookmark").Select
   Selection.InsertAfter (rs!FirstName + " " + rs!Lastname
+ " " + rs!Telephone)
  Selection.Collapse
End If
rs.Close
db.Close
End Sub
```

You can also use this code in Excel or other applications that use VBA.

Now return to the Word document and run the macro. The first name and telephone number appears at the bookmarked point in the document.

Investigate the MoveNext and FindFirst recordset methods to see how to create more advanced data access macros – e.g. to print a complete address list.

This data was entered automatically from the SPORTS.MDB database.

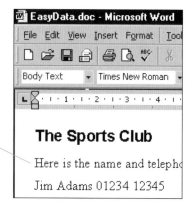

Programming the Office Assistant

The jaunty paperclip and Power Pup are annoying to some, and a cheerful way to get help for others. If you enjoy the Office Assistant, here is how you can control it in your Visual Basic code. It is an adaptation of the dialog example on the previous page, except this time the Assistant is used instead of a custom dialog.

The Assistant is an easy, quick way to create dialogs, but not as flexible as a custom form.

1 Return to the document containing the DocStart macro and open Visual Basic. Double-click the module containing DocStart, and edit the procedure so it looks like this:

```
Sub DocStart()
Dim OptionChosen As Integer

With Assistant
.Visible = True
.Animation =
msoAnimationGetAttentionMinor
    With .NewBalloon
    .Heading = "Start a new document"
    .Text = "Select a document type"
    .Labels(1).Text = "General document"
    .Labels(2).Text = "Letter"
    .Mode = msoModeModal
    OptionChosen = .Show
    End With
End With
'... continues as old DocStart procedure
```

Which Assistant appears depends on the user's choice in the Assistant's Options dialog.

If the user has turned off the Assistant, the macro will not work. Choose "Show the Office Assistant" from the Help menu.

2 Return to the document and run DocStart again. This time the Assistant appears. Otherwise, the macro works just as before.

More about the Assistant

Programming the Office Assistant is a good example of how Visual Basic works in Office. To create your own animated Assistant would take a long time and considerable skill, but by using the one built into Office, you can take full advantage of it very easily.

Under the surface, the Assistant is controlled by ActiveX. To make it available to Visual Basic, the Microsoft Office Object Library must be checked in the References dialog. It is checked by default if you are using Visual Basic from Word.

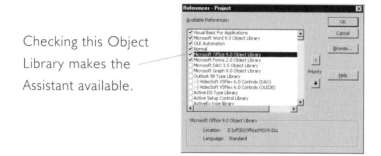

Checking this Object Library makes the Assistant available.

Once the reference has been set up, you can simply use the methods and properties of the Assistant object as if it were part of Visual Basic. The main challenge is discovering exactly what those properties and methods are. Visual Basic helps by popping up a list when you type the dot character, for example within a With Assistant block. The other great source of information is on-line help. Select the word Assistant in your code and press F1 to open the right entry.

Pop-up help   On-line help

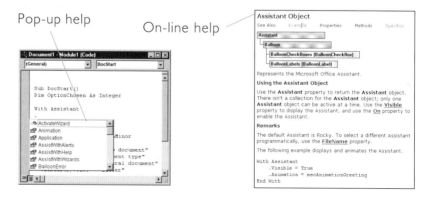

Controlling Excel from Word

Once you have successfully created macros that run within an Office application, the next step is to control one application from another. An example would be if you wanted a Word document to include information from an Excel spreadsheet.

There are other ways of linking to Excel spreadsheets from Word documents, but this is the most powerful technique since you have full control over all Excel's features.

1 To set up this example, create a workbook called Sales and include a named cell called SalesTotal. Put a suitably impressive figure in it, save the workbook and close Excel.

2 In Word, start a new document and write a document which includes a bookmark called SalesTotal. It does not need to have the same name as the Excel bookmark, that is just a convenience.

3 Use Tools > Macro > Macros > Create to start a new macro called GetSalesTotal.

4 Before adding the code for the macro, choose Tools > References from the Visual Basic menu. Check the reference for Microsoft Excel Object Library.

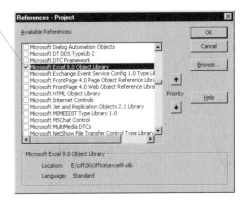

5 Now you can write code which controls Excel. The key function in the following code is CreateObject. This actually runs Excel in the background so you can then instruct it to open a workbook.

```
Sub GetSalesTotal()
Dim xl As Excel.Application
Dim sAmount As String

Set xl=CreateObject("Excel.Application")
xl.Workbooks.Open ("C:\MYDATA\SALES.XLS")
sAmount=Str(xl.ActiveSheet.Range("SalesTotal").Value)
ActiveDocument.Bookmarks("SalesTotal").Select
Selection.InsertAfter ("$" + Trim$(sAmount))
Set xl=Nothing
End Sub
```

Change the file name shown to the correct path for wherever you saved SALES.XLS.

6 Return to Word and run the macro. If your code is free of mistakes, then the sales figure will appear in the document.

Using Office from Visual Basic

You are not restricted to controlling one Office application from another. You can also control any Office application from a stand-alone Visual Basic program. In this example, the same code that was used from VBA in Word is transferred to a stand-alone Visual Basic application.

It is not only the programs in Office that can be automated. Many other software packages now support this system.

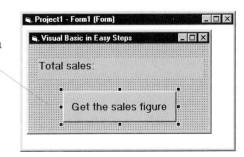

Run the full version of Visual Basic and start a new project. On the form, place a command button and a label, and set the captions as shown.

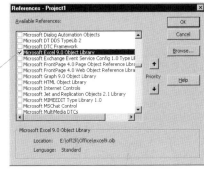

Choose References from the Project menu, and check the reference to Microsoft Excel Object Library. Then close the dialog.

See the next page for some more information about how this code works.

Double-click the command button and enter the following code for the Click event:

```
Dim xl As Excel.Application
Dim sAmount As String

Set xl=CreateObject("Excel.Application")
xl.Workbooks.Open ("C:\MYDATA\SALES.XLS")
sAmount=Str(xl.ActiveSheet.Range("SalesTotal").Value)
Label1.Caption="Total sales: " & "$" &
Trim$(sAmount)
Set xl=Nothing
```

The main snag with code like this is that running Excel in the background is a demanding task. On low-specification systems it may not work well. You should test it carefully on the target system.

4 Run the application and click the button. Visual Basic retrieves the value from the SALES.XLS workbook and displays it in the label control.

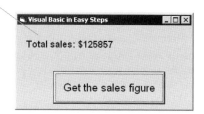

Tips on using Office from Visual Basic

If you look at the code for controlling another application, you can see four stages:

1. DIM the object variable. You should always use a specific declaration like "As Excel.Application" rather than the generic "As Object". This is because performance will be better.

One point that can be confusing at first is that automated objects are started invisibly. If you want the user to see the application running, or interact with it, you must set its visible property to True.

2. SET the object variable to point to an instance of the object. Visual Basic has two alternative functions for this. CreateObject generally starts a new instance. For example, it will run a second instance of Excel even if Excel is already running. GetObject, by contrast, will return an already-running instance if available. GetObject can also take a file name parameter, which saves time if you want to start the application with a file loaded.

3. Call the object's methods and properties. This is where you do the work you need.

4. SET the object variable to Nothing. This last step ensures that the application does not stay in memory when it is no longer needed. Sometimes this step may not be necessary, but it is always good practice.

Visual Basic and the Internet

Everyone seems to be on the web today, and this chapter shows how Visual Basic makes it possible to build exciting web projects. Using Visual Basic script, you can create dynamic web pages. In your Visual Basic applications, you can send emails automatically and integrate your applications with web sites.

Covers

Chapter Seven

What kind of web?

A web is any system where web browsers can view HTML pages over a network. HTML stands for Hypertext Markup Language, and it lets you easily move from one page to another by clicking "hot-links".

The best known network of this kind is the Internet, home of the World Wide Web. But there are many different ways in which web technology is used:

- You may have a private network which includes a web server. This is called an Intranet.

- You may be creating web pages for the World Wide Web, which you upload to an ISP (Internet Service Provider) to make them available for public view.

- You may be part of an organization that has a permanent link to the Internet.

Web pages are not just static documents, but can also allow you to query databases, place orders for goods, or play games. In fact, most things that can be done with traditional applications can also be done on web pages. Visual Basic's support for web features is important, as Web applications are becoming a popular alternative to standard Windows software.

A problem with the Internet is that different browser versions and computer platforms make it hard to create web pages that have the same features everywhere. If you are using an Intranet, it is easier to control what browsers your users have. Many of Visual Basic's web features only work with Internet Explorer, and not Netscape Navigator. This is OK on an Intranet but not on the World Wide Web.

Using Internet Explorer to view an Intranet page

The basics of web scripting

JavaScript is also known as JScript or EcmaScript. The reason is that the JavaScript name belongs to Netscape. JavaScript is quite different from Java, another web programming language, despite its similar name.

HTML was designed as a document format that you could view on different computer platforms and which included the ability to click on "hot-links" to move from one page to another. HTML has also developed extra features that make it possible to use it for applications, as you would use a Visual Basic form.

HTML pages are stored as simple text together with tags, keywords in angle brackets, that have special meaning to the web browser, or in some cases to the web server on which the pages are stored.

Even early versions of HTML support simple forms with checkboxes, text fields and buttons. Before web scripts were introduced, almost the only thing such forms could do was to send the contents of the completed form to a web server for processing. When scripting was added, it was possible to run scripts as well, short programs which run on the web browser's system to automate a process or to provide dynamic content or animation.

VB Script and JavaScript

A simple rule of thumb is that you should use JavaScript if you want scripts to run on browsers over the World Wide Web. If you are developing an Intranet where everyone uses Internet Explorer, then using VB Script is no problem.

There are two widely used scripting languages for web pages. VB (Visual Basic) Script was designed by Microsoft and is similar to the full Visual Basic, but with cut-down features. Visual Basic Script is supported by Microsoft Internet Explorer 3.0 and later versions. JavaScript was designed by Netscape and is supported by both Internet Explorer and Netscape Navigator.

Despite the above, it is possible to use VB Script and have web pages viewed by Netscape Navigator. You do this by running the scripts on the web server and not on the browser. See page 158 for more information.

A first web page script

Run Notepad. Type in the script as shown.

This is HTML header information, necessary for web browsers to recognize the file as proper HTML.

This indicates the start of an HTML form.

Don't forget to include the SCRIPT LANGUAGE="VBS" instruction. Otherwise, the browser will assume it is JavaScript and report errors.

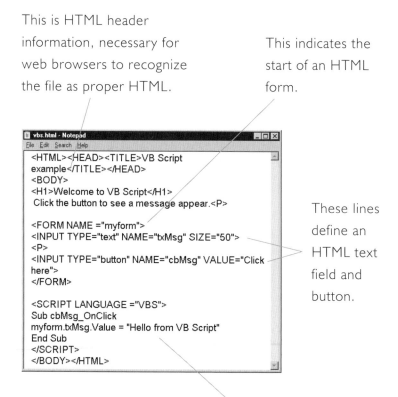

These lines define an HTML text field and button.

This is the VB Script subroutine. The name of the procedure determines when it runs.

You do not need Visual Basic installed to run this example. Just Internet Explorer will do.

2 Save the script as C:\VBS.HTML. Then run Internet Explorer, type C:\VBS.HTML in the address box, and press Enter. Click the button to try the script.

More about VB Script

In HTML, closing tags are the same as opening tags, but with a "/" prefix.

Where to place VB Script

You can include VB Script anywhere on a web page as long as it is enclosed in an opening and closing <SCRIPT> tag, with the language set to "VBS" as in the example on the previous page.

How to write script that responds to events

You create scripts that respond to events by naming the procedure according to the event. The rule is that if the procedure is called:

There are other ways to connect events to scripts, but this is the easiest to start with.

```
Sub MyObject_MyEvent
```

then it will run whenever MyEvent occurs for MyObject. HTML buttons have an onClick event, so a routine to respond to a button click is called:

```
Sub MyButton_onClick
```

What events are available?

The following table lists common events which work with most HTML controls. Many other events are available for particular objects and browsers.

VB Script is a subset of the full Visual Basic. For security reasons, it lacks functions to read and write files. All variables are of the variant type, and you cannot call the Windows API. There are many other differences, but the fundamentals of the language are the same.

onBlur	Object loses focus
onChange	Text changes
onClick	Object is clicked
onFocus	Object gets focus
onSelect	Text is selected
onMouseOver	Mouse passes over object
onSubmit	Form is submitted

How do you create global variables?

Declare a variable with Dim outside a procedure to make it visible throughout the <SCRIPT> block. Declare it with Public to make it visible to all scripts in the document.

A VBScript quiz example

HTML is not case-sensitive, so you can use `<form>` instead of `<FORM>` if you like.

This example uses several VB Script techniques, including a script-level variable, radio buttons, and an "if - then" condition. As with the last example, the script is created in Notepad, saved as a file with an .HTM or .HTML extension, and run by opening it in Internet Explorer.

1 The first part of the script begins with an HTML header as in the previous example.

2 This part of the form will be rendered as text, with the `<H1>` tag indicating a heading.

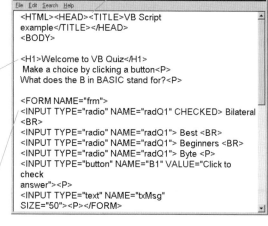

```
vbquiz.html - Notepad
File  Edit  Search  Help
<HTML><HEAD><TITLE>VB Script
example</TITLE></HEAD>
<BODY>

<H1>Welcome to VB Quiz</H1>
 Make a choice by clicking a button<P>
What does the B in BASIC stand for?<P>

<FORM NAME="frm">
<INPUT TYPE="radio" NAME="radQ1" CHECKED> Bilateral
<BR>
<INPUT TYPE="radio" NAME="radQ1"> Best <BR>
<INPUT TYPE="radio" NAME="radQ1"> Beginners <BR>
<INPUT TYPE="radio" NAME="radQ1"> Byte <P>
<INPUT TYPE="button" NAME="B1" VALUE="Click to
check
answer"><P>
<INPUT TYPE="text" NAME="txMsg"
SIZE="50"><P></FORM>
```

Working with Notepad is rough-and-ready compared to Visual Basic's slick editor. You can have similar facilities when creating scripts, for example with Microsoft Visual InterDev. See page 158.

3 Next, a form is defined. INPUT TYPE="radio" defines a radio button. The NAME attribute is important – all radio buttons with the same name are in the same group. When you check one, any other checked button will automatically become unchecked. The CHECKED attribute means it is checked when first displayed.

4 Two additional INPUT controls define a button and a text area respectively. The button will be used to find out whether the answer is correct, and the text area to display a message.

5 The next part of the document is the Visual Basic script. It begins by defining a variable outside any procedure. This makes it a script-level variable that remains visible and valid after the procedure runs.

HTML radio buttons are counted from 0, so Item(2) is the third radio button in the group.

 This key line tests the Checked property of the third radio button.

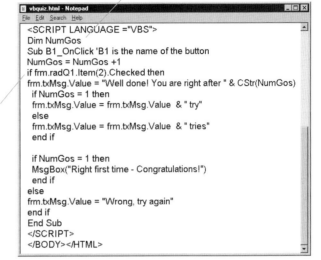

```
vbquiz.html - Notepad
File  Edit  Search  Help
<SCRIPT LANGUAGE ="VBS">
Dim NumGos
Sub B1_OnClick 'B1 is the name of the button
NumGos = NumGos +1
if frm.radQ1.Item(2).Checked then
frm.txMsg.Value = "Well done! You are right after " & CStr(NumGos)
  if NumGos = 1 then
  frm.txMsg.Value = frm.txMsg.Value  & " try"
  else
  frm.txMsg.Value = frm.txMsg.Value  & " tries"
  end if

  if NumGos = 1 then
  MsgBox("Right first time - Congratulations!")
  end if
else
frm.txMsg.Value = "Wrong, try again"
end if
End Sub
</SCRIPT>
</BODY></HTML>
```

You can use MsgBox even within an HTML script.

VB Script only works in Internet Explorer, so do not try this with Netscape Navigator. For that, use JavaScript instead.

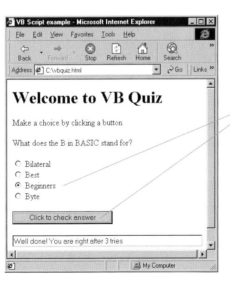

7 View the page in Internet Explorer to try the quiz. Check a choice and then click the button.

Scripting the Explorer object

One of the most useful features of VB Script is that you can program Internet Explorer itself. You do not need to take any special steps. In your code, simply refer to built-in objects like Window, Document and Navigator. Try the following techniques:

This script detects the browser version and displays a message when the page loads:

You can also inspect the code name and user agent of the browser, in the appCodeName and UserAgent properties.

```
Sub Window_OnLoad
frm.txBrowser.Value = Navigator.AppName & " " &
Navigator.AppVersion
msgbox "Welcome to my web page"
End Sub
```

To program a color, you can either specify a color name, or a code giving a hexadecimal value like #FFFF00.

This script changes the background color of the page:

```
Sub cbChangeColor_Onclick
Document.BgColor = "fuschia"
End Sub
```

To make these scripts work, you need to add buttons with matching names, as in the complete examples on pages 142–143.

This script displays a prompt and then navigates to the chosen destination.

```
Sub cbGoSomewhere_OnClick
NewInput = Window.Prompt("Navigate to
where?","C:\VBQUIZ.HTML")
   if NewInput <> "" then
  Window.Navigate(NewInput)
  end if
end sub
```

A Web location is called a URL, which stands for Uniform Resource Locator. This can be a file as well as a web location, but only if you are running the browser on the same network as the file.

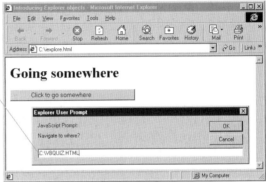

This script opens a new Explorer Window at a chosen location.

```
Sub cbOpenWindow_OnClick
window.open "C:\VBQUIZ.HTML","MyNewWin"
End Sub
```

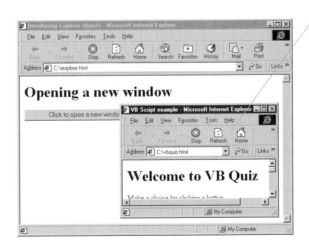

Scripting ActiveX and Java

Internet Explorer is able to include ActiveX controls on web pages. You can code these from VB Script, for exceptional power and performance. Performance is good because the ActiveX control runs as native code on the user's system. The disadvantage is that the control must be installed and registered first. It is best to use ActiveX controls on an Intranet, where you can be sure users already have the ActiveX controls they need.

How to include an ActiveX Control

Every ActiveX control has a unique number which identifies it. In the full Visual Basic, this number is hidden from you, but because a HTML page is a plain text document, the number has to appear in the text. It will not normally be visible to users browsing your page. There are also tools to let you insert the number without typing it in.

The basics of using ActiveX Controls in web pages are simple. The <OBJECT> tag has a CLASSID attribute, which is the number identifying the control. After that, properties, methods and events work in the same way as for other controls like buttons. It is difficult to discover the correct CLASSID by hand, so it is best to use a tool which looks it up for you.

You will find it much easier to work with ActiveX controls if you have a web authoring tool which supports them, such as Microsoft FrontPage.

This script includes an ActiveX calendar control (see opposite)

```
<HTML> <HEAD><TITLE>
ActiveX example</TITLE></HEAD><BODY>
<H1>ActiveX Scripting Example</H1>
This is an ActiveX control:<P>
<FORM NAME="frm">

<OBJECT ID="Calendar1"
CLASSID="CLSID:8E27C92B-1264-101C-8A2F-040224009C02"
width="288" height="192"></OBJECT>

<p><input type="text" name="T1" size="50"></p>
<p>
<p>Click on a date to see what is happening that day.</p>
</FORM>
</p>

<SCRIPT LANGUAGE="VBS">
Sub Calendar1_Click
frm.T1.Value = frm.Calendar1.Day & "/" & frm.Calendar1.Month &
": Learn Visual Basic in Easy Steps"
End sub
</SCRIPT>

</BODY></HTML>
```

ActiveX scripting only works with Internet Explorer.

This is how the HTML on the previous page looks when displayed in a browser. Notice how the long number in the CLASSID attribute has become a fancy visual control.

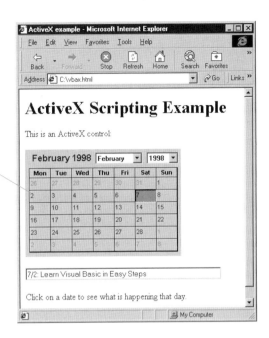

Scripting Java

For an applet to be scriptable, it must have public methods and properties.

You can also use VB Script to control Java applets. These have some degree of similarity to ActiveX controls, and are included using the <APPLET> tag instead of the <OBJECT> tag. If they are designed to be scripted, they can be scripted in a similar way to ActiveX controls. Applets have several important advantages. First, they do not need to be registered on the browser's system (although they do need to be downloaded). Second, they run on Netscape Navigator as well as Internet Explorer, and on platforms such as Unix and Macintosh as well as Windows. Third, they are safer, thanks to security features in the Java language.

A problem with Java is that you need Java programming skills to assemble applets, whereas an ActiveX control can be created with Visual Basic. A second problem is that Java applets tend to run more slowly than ActiveX controls, and unlike applets ActiveX controls can use all the features of Windows.

Introducing Dynamic HTML

There are many more features in Dynamic HTML than can be described here. This is just to show how your Visual Basic skills can be put to good use on dynamic web pages.

Versions of Microsoft Internet Explorer after and including 4.0 use Dynamic HTML, a significant advance over the HTML standard in Internet Explorer 3.0. The reason is that in Dynamic HTML a web page has a Document Object Model, which means that every element can be identified and scripted.

The following example shows one way of using Visual Basic to change the text of a web page dynamically. It uses the <SPAN> tag to identify a section of text with a name. This makes that section of text a programmable object. The code writes to the innerHTML property of this object, and in doing so changes the text. There is also an innerText property, but the advantage of innerHTML is that you can include formatting as well as text.

A Dynamic Text example

This example displays a new quote when you click the button.

Another tag called <DIV> is similar to <SPAN> but works at a higher level. You can group several <SPAN> sections within one <DIV> section.

1 Including text within the <SPAN> tag makes this part of the document into an object that you can use in your script.

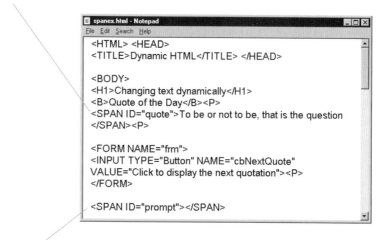

2 This second <SPAN> section has no text at all when the page first loads.

A good way to progress with scripting Dynamic HTML is to obtain Microsoft Visual InterDev, which includes a complete online reference.

3 This script has a script level variable to let you cycle through quotes. The OnClick procedure displays the quote that matches the number, and then increases the number or resets it to zero. The quote is displayed by setting the innerHTML property of the <SPAN> object.

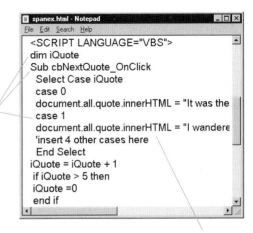

```
spanex.html - Notepad
File  Edit  Search  Help
<SCRIPT LANGUAGE="VBS">
dim iQuote
Sub cbNextQuote_OnClick
  Select Case iQuote
  case 0
  document.all.quote.innerHTML = "It was the
  case 1
  document.all.quote.innerHTML = "I wandere
  'insert 4 other cases here
  End Select
iQuote = iQuote + 1
if iQuote > 5 then
  iQuote =0
  end if
```

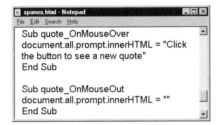

```
spanex.html - Notepad
File  Edit  Search  Help
Sub quote_OnMouseOver
document.all.prompt.innerHTML = "Click
the button to see a new quote"
End Sub

Sub quote_OnMouseOut
document.all.prompt.innerHTML = ""
End Sub
```

4 This code displays a prompt when the mouse is over a quotation, and removes it when the mouse moves elsewhere.

You can also display tooltips in a web page, by giving objects a TITLE attribute.

5 Test your work by opening the page in Internet Explorer. Click the button to show a new quote. Move the mouse to show the prompt.

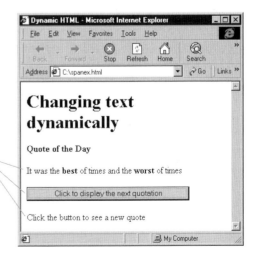

Changing text dynamically

Quote of the Day

It was the **best** of times and the **worst** of times

Click to display the next quotation

Click the button to see a new quote

Using a web timer for animation

The most dynamic web pages are those which are active even when the user is not clicking the mouse. You can easily achieve this using Internet Explorer's built-in timer.

The one thing to be careful about is that the timer procedure must not take too long to execute. If you loaded large graphic files, for example, the effect would be frustrating rather than impressive.

The way it works is that when the page loads, you call the browser window's setInterval method, passing the name of another procedure as the parameter, along with a time interval in milliseconds. The timer then calls that procedure repeatedly, at the requested time interval. In your procedure you can load images, create text effects, in fact do anything that VB Script allows.

A timer example

This script is quite similar to the one on the previous page, so not all of it is shown.

Use <SPAN> to set up a text object. This will contain a changing message. Note the use of the FONT SIZE tag to obtain a large font.

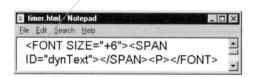

```
timer.html - Notepad
File  Edit  Search  Help
<FONT SIZE="+6"><SPAN
ID="dynText"></SPAN><P></FONT>
```

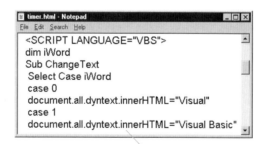

```
timer.html - Notepad
File  Edit  Search  Help
<SCRIPT LANGUAGE="VBS">
dim iWord
Sub ChangeText
Select Case iWord
case 0
document.all.dyntext.innerHTML="Visual"
case 1
document.all.dyntext.innerHTML="Visual Basic"
```

2 Write a ChangeText procedure which changes the text each time it is called. This example gradually reveals a message. Note the use once again of a script level variable.

Adjust the second parameter to change the speed at which the message displays.

3 This is the key bit of code. When the document loads, this event fires, calling the SetInterval function. The first parameter is the name of your ChangeText procedure. The second is the number of milliseconds between calls.

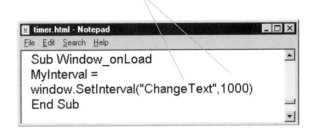

A snag with animated text is that it can be distracting or irritating. It is a good idea to reserve this kind of effect for pages which do not require concentration! You can be sure your message will be noticed.

4 Load the page in Internet Explorer to see the results. The message builds up gradually, starting the cycle again when it is complete, for a truly dynamic effect.

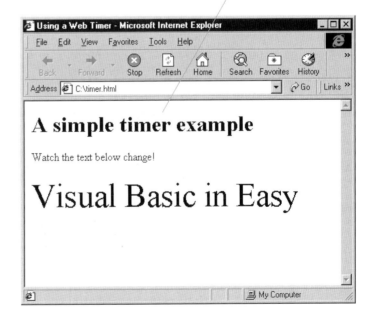

Creating a custom web browser

If you prefer to pass control to the user's own browser rather than embedding it into an application, see page 154.

A remarkable feature of Internet Explorer is that its main engine, the part which interprets and displays web pages, can be embedded into your own Visual Basic application.

Start a new Visual Basic project and right-click the Toolbox to open the Components dialog. Check Microsoft Internet Controls and close the dialog with OK.

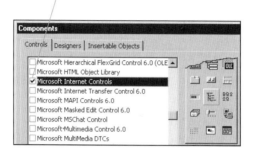

2 Select the Web Browser component that has appeared on the Toolbox and place it on a form. Stretch it out to nearly fill the form. Above it, place a text box and a button.

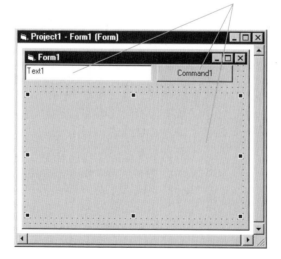

3 Give the button a caption of say, "Go there", and enter the following code for its Click event:

```
WebBrowser1.Navigate Text1.Text
```

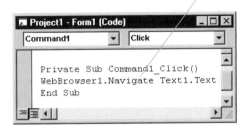

4 Run the application, enter a web address in the text box, and click the "Go there" button.

5 To improve the application, add some code to the Form's resize event so that when you resize the form at runtime, the browser control resizes with it. This assumes a layout like that on the previous page. Note the use of the ScaleWidth and ScaleHeight properties, which measure the internal area of the form.

```
Private Sub Form_Resize()
WebBrowser1.Top = Text1.Height
WebBrowser1.Width = Form1.ScaleWidth
WebBrowser1.Height = Form1.ScaleHeight -
Text1.Height
End Sub
```

Using ShellExecute for web features

The previous example showed how to include a web browser object in an application, but often it is preferable to make a web page appear in the user's normal browser. Then the user gets all the toolbars and menus of their browser as well as the web page itself.

Another common requirement is to open the user's email application with an email address already in place.

Both these can be easily done using an API (Application Programming Interface) function called ShellExecute. To use it, you need to include its declaration in a code module.

Start a new Visual Basic project and choose Project>Add module to insert a code module. Next, choose Add-ins>API Viewer and load WIN32API.TXT from its File menu. Ensure the API Type dropdown shows Declares, type in Shell, and select ShellExecute from the list. Click Add to put the declaration in the bottom text area, and then Copy to copy it to the clipboard.

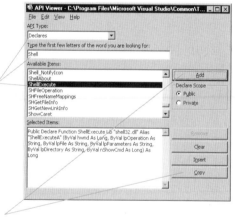

2 Now open the code module and choose Edit>Paste.

...cont'd

This API function has many options which you can look up in online help. You should also test the return value to see if an error has occurred.

3 Open the project's form and lay it out with text boxes and buttons as shown. The first button will open a web page at the given address, while the second will start an email to the address shown.

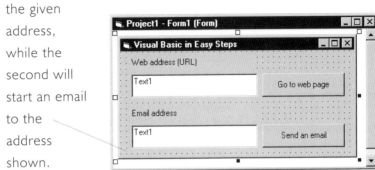

4 Add the following code for the first button's Click event:

```
Dim iRetVal As Integer
iRetVal = ShellExecute(Form1.hwnd, "open",
Text1.Text, vbNull, vbNull, 0)
```
and for the second button:
```
Dim iRetVal As Integer
Dim sEmail As String
sEmail = "mailto: " + Text2.Text
iRetVal = ShellExecute(Form1.hwnd, "open",
sEmail, vbNull, vbNull, 0)
```

When you type this, note that the last two lines in each procedure should be typed on a single line.

5 Run the application to test it with some example addresses.

For this to work, you must add the right prefix to the addresses. Web addresses start "http://" while email addresses start "mailto:" It is these prefixes that tell Windows which application to run.

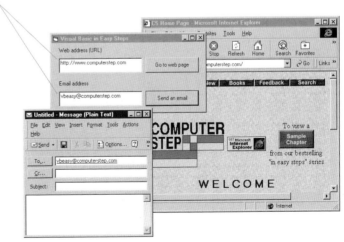

Advanced email: VB and MAPI

The technique shown on the previous page is fine for starting off an email message, but it is not fully automated. What if you wanted your software to automatically generate and send an email message, with a subject and text as well as an address?

The full details of the MAPI specification are complex. Use this as a simple example, but look up the online reference for full details of how to use the MAPI controls.

To do this you need to go a stage further. Visual Basic comes with a couple of controls called MAPI, which stands for Mail Application Programming Interface. Using these controls, you can automate the whole email process, so long as you have a MAPI-complaint email application already installed. Microsoft's Outlook and Outlook Express are both suitable.

1 Start a new Visual Basic project. On the toolbox, right-click and choose Components. Find and check the Microsoft MAPI controls and close the dialog with OK.

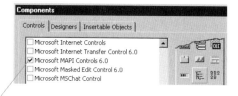

2 On the project's form, place a button and one of each of the MAPI controls: MAPISession and MAPIMessages.

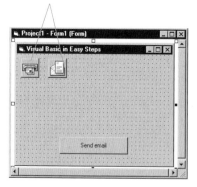

3 Here is the code for the button's Click event:

```
On Error GoTo mailerr:
MAPISession1.SignOn
If MAPISession1.SessionID <> 0 Then

With MAPIMessages1
.SessionID = MAPISession1.SessionID
.Compose ' start a new message
.RecipDisplayName = "My best friend"
.RecipAddress = "richard@myipdomain.com"
.MsgSubject = "A direct message from VB"
.MsgNoteText = "Hi Richard, hello"
.Send False ' don't display a dialog
End With
MsgBox "Message sent"
Exit Sub
End If
mailerr:
MsgBox "Error " & Err.Description
```

On some systems you may also need to set the MapiSession's Username and Password properties.

4 Run the application (amended with an email address of your choice) and then click the button. Next, open your email client to see the message. It will either be in the outbox, or in the place

The MAPI controls are also able to collect email messages, with the Fetch method.

used by your email client for sent messages.

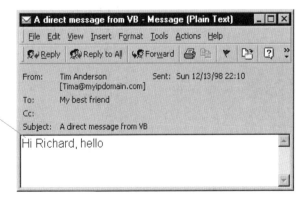

Introducing Visual InterDev

To progress with many of the topics in this chapter, such as scripting web pages or creating dynamic web sites with Visual Basic, you may want to obtain Microsoft Visual InterDev. This is part of the Visual Studio bundle, which also contains a version of Visual Basic.

Visual InterDev lets you run scripts in a debugger, which is a great advantage when building complex pages. Its primary function though is as a tool for developing Active Server Pages, a technique whereby scripts (including VB Script) can be run on a web server, while presenting pure HTML to the browsers. That means you can code a web site with Visual Basic and remain compatible with every kind of web browser, including Netscape Navigator.

Using Visual InterDev, you can explore some interesting projects like web pages that return data directly from a database to the Web.

Microsoft has another web page designer called FrontPage. FrontPage is good for visual design, but for programming the Web Visual InterDev is more suitable.

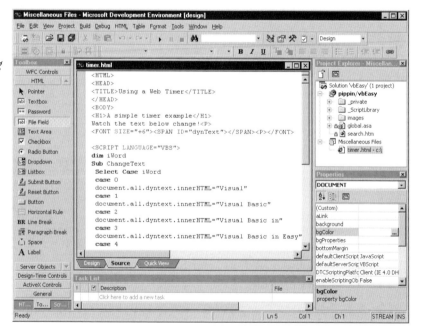

Tips for Experts

It is one thing to be able to create Visual Basic applications, and another to create good ones. This chapter explains the key concept of error-trapping, and also contains many tips for building applications that work reliably and fast.

Covers

Chapter Eight

Introducing error-trapping

Visual Basic is safer for the user than many alternative programming systems. A Visual Basic application is unlikely to cause your system to crash, for example. However, there are still plenty of reasons why errors occur. Most are caused by errors in your code, or by failing to anticipate all the ways in which your program may be used. Here is a simple example:

Visual Basic's default behavior is to stop running when an error occurs. For users this is unsatisfactory, especially if they have unsaved work at the time.

Hitting an
error in
Visual Basic

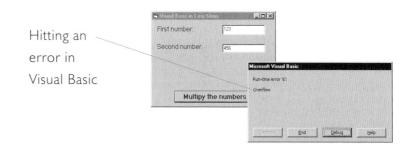

You can see the reason for the error if you see the code:

```
Dim myint As Integer
myint = Val(Text1.Text) * Val(Text2.Text)
Label1.Caption = "The answer is: " + _
    Trim(Str$(myint))
```

The variable myint is declared as an integer. This works fine with small numbers, but if the result is above 32,767, the application stops with an Error 6 – overflow message. Even if you DIM myint as a Longint, it is easy to enter a number large enough to cause an overflow.

On Error

Visual Basic's On Error statement is a solution. On Error lets you tell Visual Basic what to do if an error occurs. There are two choices:

```
On Error Resume Next
```

means ignore the error and go to the next line of code.

```
On Error Goto label
```

means go to the label specified and run the code there.

Here is how to improve the last example by adding an error handler.

The term "error-handler" means a section of code which only runs when an error has occurred. Its purpose is to recover gracefully from the problem.

This line sets up the error-handler.

This line prevents the error-handler from running when no error has occurred, by exiting the procedure before the error-handling code.

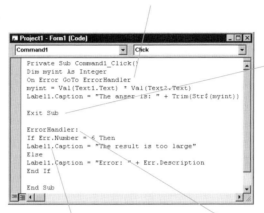

```
Project1 - Form1 (Code)
Command1                    Click
Private Sub Command1_Click()
Dim myint As Integer
On Error GoTo ErrorHandler
myint = Val(Text1.Text) * Val(Text2.Text)
Label1.Caption = "The anser is: " + Trim(Str$(myint))

Exit Sub

ErrorHandler:
If Err.Number = 6 Then
Label1.Caption = "The result is too large"
Else
Label1.Caption = "Error: " + Err.Description
End If

End Sub
```

By checking the number property of the Err object, an appropriate message is displayed.

This is the label (note the colon at the end of the word) which marks the start of the error handler.

See the next page for more about the Err object.

Trying out the error-handler

Here is what happens when you run the new code:

Instead of exiting with an obscure message, the revised application informs the user of the problem and keeps running.

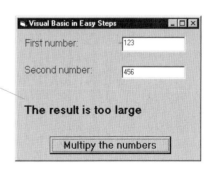

Visual Basic in Easy Steps

First number: 123

Second number: 456

The result is too large

Multipy the numbers

More about the Err object

Visual Basic has a built-in error object called Err. When an error occurs, details of the error are put into the properties of the Err object, so that your error-handling code can find out which error occurred and respond accordingly.

The key property of Err is Number. Each runtime error in Visual Basic has an unique number. If you look at the entry called Trappable Errors in Visual Basic on-line help, you can see the main list. Other errors, such as those for data access, are in separate lists.

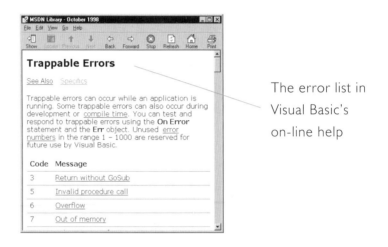

The error list in Visual Basic's on-line help

Good error messages are clear, avoid technical language, and explain what the user needs to do next. It can also be helpful to include a telephone number for technical support.

Another useful property of the Err object is Description. Numbers are little use unless you have the Visual Basic documentation to hand. The Description property is a short phrase describing the error. It is better than nothing, but even this is not likely to mean much to the user. In the example on the previous page, the Description property returns the single word Overflow. It is better to write code that checks for the most likely errors and displays a more friendly message.

Sometimes, an error-handler does not need to display a message. In some cases, the error may not be significant, or you can write code that successfully recovers from the error without the user needing to know about it. Some code even depends on error-handling to work, although this is not the best approach in most cases.

Helping the user

One of the best ways to avoid errors is by making it hard for the user to make mistakes.

1. Use the Enabled and Visible properties

Set the Visible property for options that are completely irrelevant to the current state of the application. Set the Enabled property to give the user a clue that, if something else happens, that option will become available. For example, Edit>Cut is a good candidate for enabling and disabling rather than hiding completely.

Most applications have buttons and menu options which are not always relevant. Worse, if used at the wrong moment they might cause an error. For example, you might have a Close option which closes a document. If there is no document open, Close means nothing.

The solution is to either to hide or disable irrelevant or dangerous options. In your Open code, you could have a line like this:

```
mnuFileClose.Enabled = True
```

When the last document is closed, you can have:

```
mnuFileClose.Enabled = False
```

If you prefer to remove the option completely, use the Visible property.

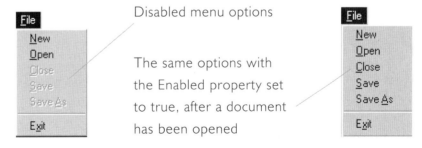

Disabled menu options

The same options with the Enabled property set to true, after a document has been opened

2. Use help tips, progress bars and status bars

To change the shape of the mouse-pointer, set the MousePointer property for a form, a control, or for the Screen object. See on-line help for the possible values.

Instant help text that appears when an option is selected, or when the mouse is over a control, is a great help to the user. Many controls have a ToolTipText property.

If an operation takes a significant amount of time, set the mouse pointer to an hourglass and show progress in a status bar or progress bar whenever possible. Users need to see something happening, in case they assume the application has crashed.

How to organize your code

As soon as your applications are more than trivial, you will need to think carefully about how to organize your code. One question is when to use a function or procedure. User-defined functions and procedures have the effect of breaking up your code into smaller chunks. There are three main reasons to use them.

- When you would otherwise repeat the same section of code at several points in your application. If you are tempted to copy and paste code from another part of the project, consider using a function or procedure instead. Repeated code is error-prone, since you might later on amend one copy of the code but not the other.

- To avoid long blocks of code. Longer blocks of code are harder to read and therefore more error-prone.

- To make it easier to maintain and improve the code. For example, imagine you have a charting feature that draws a chart, called by both a menu option and a toolbar button. You could put all the code in the Click event for both these controls, but that is inefficient. It is better to have a DrawChart procedure which you can call from both click events. DrawChart could be in the general section of a form, or better still in a separate code module. If you later want to improve the chart-drawing code, you will know exactly where to find it in the project.

One advantage of using a separate code module is that you can build up a library of your own functions, which you can use in many different projects.

This has all the code in one Click procedure.

Here, the real work has moved to a separate procedure, called from the Click event.

Tips for readable code

When you are enthusiastic about a project, it is easy to bang out lines and lines of code. Later on, when you come to correct or improve the code, it is important to be able to find your way around easily. Here are some tips.

1. Use plenty of white space

The names you choose for functions, procedures and variables also make a difference to readability. See the next page for some tips.

When Visual Basic runs your project, the white space, in the form of blank lines and indents, is ignored. You can take advantage of that by using it generously in your code. Separate your functions into logical blocks and use one or two blank lines between them.

2. Indent carefully

Indentation is even more important. It is easy to get confused by long, multi-level If or Select Case blocks. Make a point of indenting each new level, and of doing so in a consistent way throughout your code.

Use blank lines and indentation to make it easy to see the structure of If blocks

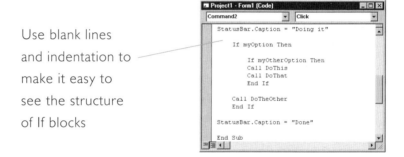

Any line that begins with a single quote mark is a comment. You can also add comments to the end of a line, following a single quote character.

3. Comment generously

Like white space, comments are ignored at runtime so they do not slow down your code.

Ideally, comment each function and procedure to show what they do. If you are working in a team, show when they were written, and when, and who by, and when last amended. If there are parameters, say what they are for.

If you add some code to work around a problem, add a comment to explain why that code was added. Otherwise, you or someone else may come along later, not know why it is there, and delete it.

Choosing descriptive names

The names you choose for functions, procedures and variables make no difference at runtime. They do, however, make a difference to the readability of your code. Professional programmers have been known to deliberately obscure their code, simply by changing all the names to meaningless ones. More often, though, programmers want to make code easy to understand.

1. Use descriptive names

It is better to have names that are descriptive rather than short. Better to have a function called:

```
GetIncomeFromEmployeeId(EmployeeID as Long)
```

than this concise alternative:

```
GetInc(ID as Long)
```

Visual Basic is not case-sensitive, but you can make good use of upper and lower case in the names you choose.

2. Use a naming convention

Programmers love to argue about what is the best way to choose names. Schemes for devising names are called naming conventions. For example, it is useful to identify the type of an object or variable by using a consistent prefix, e.g.:

strSomething	for a string
iSomething	for an integer
sglSomething	for a single
txtSomething	for a text box

The advantage of this approach is that you are less likely to try things that cause errors, like storing a floating-point number in an integer variable.

In this book, the examples often use the default Visual Basic names for controls, like Command1 and Label1. This is fine for short examples, but in large projects it is likely to confuse. You will have lots of forms with controls called Command1 and Label1, and tracing through the code will not be easy.

Tips for fast applications

However fast your PC may be, it is still worth considering the performance of your application. That is doubly true if you distribute your work to others, since some will have slow systems. Here are some key tips.

Use Option Explicit to ensure that all variables are declared. Check Require Variable Declaration in Tools>Options.

1. Declare all variables

Variables which are not declared with Dim are invisibly declared as Variants by Visual Basic. Variants are slower to process than other kinds of variable. The single most important thing you can do to speed up projects is to Dim all variables, and use the appropriate type in every case.

This little application calculates prime numbers. The upper example runs at more than three times the speed of the bottom one. The code is identical, except that in the slow version none of the variables are declared.

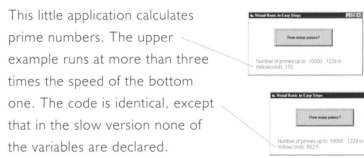

Where you can, use integers rather than floating-point numbers. Integers are faster for the computer to process.

2. Minimize usage of ActiveX controls

ActiveX controls can run fast, but they are slow to load. Another problem is that larger ActiveX controls probably have more features than you need. To keep your application slim and fast, only use ActiveX controls when you really need them.

Speed is not the only factor. Productivity counts as well. Sometimes getting reliable code written quickly is more important than performance.

3. Avoid picture boxes when you can

Although a picture box looks similar to an image control, it is internally a full-featured but heavyweight control. Image controls are more efficient.

4. Do not use a control when code will do

There are two ways to draw a line or shape on a form. One is by using a line or shape control. The other is to use the form's graphics methods, like Line and Circle. The second way is much faster.

Managing multiple forms

Most of the examples in this book have only used one form. To build a complete application, you will often find that you need more than one form. Here is how you include additional forms in your project.

1 From the Project menu, choose Add Form.

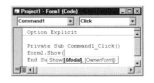

2 Choose what kind of form to add. There are a number of wizards and templates to choose from. Here, a standard form is chosen.

Should you close a form with Hide or Unload? Although both close a form, they do different things. Hide leaves the form in memory, so it is good if you need to refer to the values of its controls, or will be displaying it again soon. Unload removes the form from memory and is good if you want to conserve system resources.

3 In your code, use the new form's Show method to display the form. Show takes two parameters. The first is vbModal or vbModeless, and determines whether the application waits for the form to be closed before allowing any other actions.

4 You can close the form at runtime either by allowing the user to click the Close button at top-right, or in code with the Unload command or the Hide method.

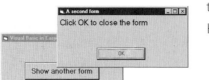

Introducing MDI

Applications which use multiple forms can get untidy, especially if the forms are displayed non-modally. If there are several applications open, it can even be hard to tell which form belongs to which application.

MDI stands for Multiple Document Interface. It is a way of managing multiple windows by trapping them within a master window. In Visual Basic, this master window is called an MDI form. Then, forms can be displayed as MDI clients, which can be moved within the master form, but not outside it. Most word-processors and spreadsheets are MDI applications.

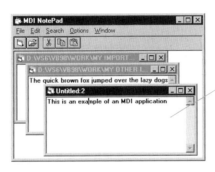

An MDI application encloses one or more forms. This is one of the examples supplied with Visual Basic.

One of the options in the Visual Basic application wizard is an MDI application.

Working with MDI forms

There is not enough space here for a full description of MDI. Getting started is easy though. First, begin a new application. Then choose Add MDI form from the project menu. Next, change the MDI property of the first form to MDIChild. When you run the form, the MDI form will appear with the MDI child form within it.

MDI forms have some special features. You cannot place controls directly on an MDI form, except for picture boxes and custom controls which have an align property. These controls align themselves to one side for use as a toolbar or status bar. You can also add menu items.

The main challenge of MDI applications is to ensure that the right child window is targeted by any code which runs. MDI forms have an ActiveForm property which identifies the currently active form.

Using Sub Main

You have to create Sub Main yourself. First, add a code module to the project. Then, add a procedure to the module called Sub Main. Typically, it will include a command to show a form.

All Visual Basic projects have a startup object. This determines which code runs first when the project opens. The startup object is set in Project Properties, and can either be one of the forms in the project (by default it is the first form), or else a procedure with the special name of Sub Main.

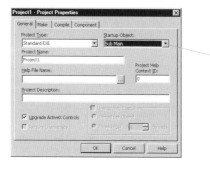

Click here to set Sub Main instead of a startup form.

Why use Sub Main?

In an application which is more than trivial, using Sub Main has several advantages. It is a convenient place to set variables to default values, open a database, or check that all the files needed by the application exist. Then you can display the initial form using its Show method.

You do not have to use Sub Main to display a splash screen. The only time you have to use Sub Main is if your application does not contain any forms. It is tidier, though, to put application start-up code in Sub Main, and reserve the form's Load event for code specific to the form.

Including a Splash screen

Starting with Sub Main makes it easy to display a splash screen. This is a form which shows while your application starts up. If the full application takes a while to load, the splash screen reassures the user that all is well. Simply include a line like:

```
frmSplash.show
DoEvents ' allows the form to be painted
```

at the beginning of Sub Main. When you have done all the initialization, continue with

```
unload frmSplash
form1.show
```

How to read a disk file

Most real-world applications need to read and write disk files. In many cases this is done for you behind the scenes. For example, if you use Visual Basic's database features, then the disk access is handled by the database engine. You do not need to worry about opening or closing disk files directly.

This example does not teach all you need to know about reading files. It does, however, show how easy it is to get started. See the next page for how to write to a file.

Even so, knowing to read and write information on a disk is a valuable skill. For example, you might want to write and display a log file. This sample shows how you can load a text file into a window.

1. Start a new application, and on the form put a text box and a command button. The Text Box has its Scrollbars property set to Vertical and Multiline set to True.

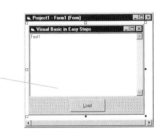

This is how the code works. Visual Basic identifies open files with a number. FreeFile returns a spare number. Open... for Input opens a file for reading. Next, the Input function reads the file and returns a string. LOF is used to measure the length of the file, so that Input can be instructed to read all of it. Finally, Close # closes the file.

2. Add this code for the button's Click event (you may need to amend the fourth line depending on the name of your Windows directory):

```
On Error GoTo ErrorHandler
Dim FileNum As Integer
FileNum = FreeFile
Open "C:\WINDOWS\WIN.INI" For Input As #FileNum
Text1.Text = Input(LOF(FileNum), #FileNum)
Close #FileNum
Exit Sub
ErrorHandler:
MsgBox "Error: "  & Err.Description
```

3. Run the project and click the button. WIN.INI displays in the window.

How to write to a file

Code for writing to a file looks similar to code for reading it. In fact, once a file is open in read/write mode, you can read and write to it as required.

Creating a log file

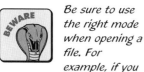

Be sure to use the right mode when opening a file. For example, if you want to read binary data like a bitmap image, you need to Open... for Binary. You can also specify whether the file is open for read-only, write-only, or read-write.

This example creates a log file which includes an entry showing the date and time when the application is started or closed.

1 Start a new application and in the form's Load event insert the following code:

```
On Error GoTo ErrorHandler
Dim FileNum As Integer
FileNum = FreeFile
Open "C:\EASYSTEP.LOG" For Append As #FileNum
Print #FileNum, "Application started: " & Str$(Now)
Close #FileNum
Exit Sub
ErrorHandler:
MsgBox "Error: " & Err.Description
```

2 Open the form's unload event and insert the same code, but replace the line beginning Print with this one:

```
Print #FileNum, "Application closed: " & Str$(Now)
```

This project is a good candidate for a user-defined procedure. Try creating a WritetoLog procedure which takes the string to be written as a parameter.

This example creates the log file the first time it is run. After that, the details are appended. If you Open... for Output, then any existing file of that name will be deleted.

This project uses the code above to write a log file, and the code from the previous example to view the log in a text box.

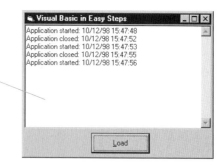

Drawing graphics

Users rightly expect Windows applications to display information graphically. So how do you draw a chart or graph? One way is to use an ActiveX control, or to embed an Excel chart into an OLE control. Although the results can be good, there is another approach. Using Visual Basic's graphic methods, you can draw your own charts and graphs on forms and picture boxes. These graphics will be drawn extremely quickly, without the performance cost of involving an ActiveX control or Excel.

How to draw in a picture box

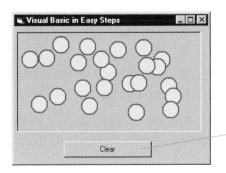

1 This example uses a form, a picture box and a button. The picture box must have its AutoRedraw property set to True. The code for the button's click event is just one line:

```
Picture1.cls
```

See the next page for more details about how this code works.

2 Place the following code in the Picture Box's MouseDown event:

```
Private Sub
Picture1_MouseDown(Button As Integer, _
  Shift As Integer, X As Single, Y As Single)
Picture1.DrawWidth = 2
Picture1.CurrentX = X
Picture1.CurrentY = Y
Picture1.FillColor = vbYellow
Picture1.FillStyle = vbSolid
Picture1.Circle Step(0, 0), 200, vbRed
End Sub
```

3 Run the project. Whenever you click on the picture box, a filled circle is drawn.

In the last example, the reason for using the event MouseDown rather than Click is that MouseDown gives you the current position of the mouse relative to the object.

The graphics methods, like those used in the last example, give you a high degree of control over what is drawn on a form or picture box. Here are some of the key properties and methods:

DrawWidth, DrawStyle

DrawWidth sets the width of the "pen" used to draw on the object. The larger the number, the thicker the lines drawn. DrawStyle sets the pattern, such as dot or dashes.

FillColor

This sets the color with which drawn objects are filled, if the FillStyle is not transparent.

FillStyle

This can be solid, transparent, or one of six styles such as vertical or diagonal lines. This lets you create graphs and charts with different hatching for each segment.

Look up the RGB function for more control over colors.

CurrentX, CurrentY

These set the coordinates which specify where the graphic is drawn.

Circle, Line

These methods draw a graphic of the type specified. The Step parameter indicates that the coordinates are relative to the CurrentX and CurrentY properties.

DrawMode

This property determines how graphics are combined when drawn – for example, when one graphic overlaps another.

To get started with graphic methods, set AutoRedraw to True.

AutoRedraw

When AutoRedraw is False, graphics are temporary, cleared the next time the image is refreshed. When it is True, the image persists. If AutoRedraw is false, you can use the Paint event to refresh the graphics as needed. By setting AutoRedraw to True, you give Visual Basic this responsibility.

Using control arrays

If you have used Visual Basic for any length of time, you will have seen the message that appears when using copy and paste to duplicate a control. Visual Basic asks, "Do you want to create a control array?" Choose Yes, and you will have two controls with the same name on the form. They are only distinguished by an index number. Here is how it works.

Using a control array

You can also use the usual keyboard shortcuts Ctrl+C and Ctrl+V to copy and paste controls.

1 Place a command button on a form, select it and choose Edit>Copy. Then choose Edit>Paste. A dialog appears asking if you want to create a control array. Click Yes.

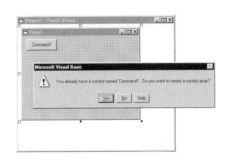

2 Choose Edit>Paste again, and another button appears. All are called Command1. If you look at the Index property in the property window, you will see that, although all three buttons have the same name, the index is different.

3 Now double-click one of the buttons to open the Click event. All three buttons share the same event code. So, to discover which button is clicked you use the Index parameter. For example:

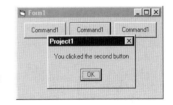

```
Select Case Index
Case 0
MsgBox "You clicked the first button"
Case 1
MsgBox "You clicked the second button"
    ' etc
```

More about control arrays

There are two reasons for using control arrays; one is obvious and one is not. The obvious reason is for coding efficiency. A good example is an address book application with a button for every letter of the alphabet. Clicking a button searches for names beginning with that letter. The code for each button is the same, apart from the letter chosen. By using a control array, you can handle all the letters in the code for one click event.

Creating controls at runtime

The other reason for using a control array is because it lets you create controls at runtime. You may want to do this if you cannot know at design time how many controls are needed. The example illustrated uses an image control, a button and a common dialog control. At runtime the user can add another icon to the form by clicking the button. There is not room to show all the code, but the essential elements are:

Buttons in a control array can have different captions, although they share the same name.

Menus can be control arrays as well. Use the Index field in the menu designer to create a menu array.

Another option is to fill a form with invisible controls, and set their visible property to True when needed. The control array is more elegant and more efficient, and lets you create exactly the number you need.

1. Use a Static variable, say NewIdx, to store the index number of the last control created.

2. To create a new image control, increase the NewIdx variable by one and use the line:

    ```
    Load Image1(newidx)
    ```

3. Position the new control by setting its top and left properties. You can position it next to the previous control by inspecting the top and left properties of Image1(newidx-1). You can tell if it would disappear off the form by checking the ScaleWidth property of the form. If so, start a new line of images. If it would disappear off the bottom, cancel the action and display a message informing the user the new icon will not fit.

4. Finally, load the icon using the common dialog control and set the image control's visible property to True.

Interrupt with DoEvents

In fact, you can usually interrupt an errant program by pressing Ctrl+Alt+Del and terminating it from the Task Manager. It is not a sign of good software, though.

Nothing is worse than accidentally triggering an option that takes a long time, and then not being able to cancel it. Of course, you can reboot the PC, but quality software should not require such drastic measures.

Now, imagine you have a procedure that performs some lengthy processing in a loop. For example, you might have a routine which calculates how many prime numbers there are in numbers up to one million. That takes significant time, even on a fast system. The problem is that while Visual Basic is racing round the code loop, the rest of the application is dead. You cannot have a Cancel button, because no click event will fire until the loop is done. Worse still, if a bug causes an infinite loop, the user will not be able to break in.

Using DoEvents

There are several ways around this problem. The simplest is to use DoEvents. This command hands control back to Windows, so that click events or other actions can be processed before the loop continues. Here is how to do it:

If you use DoEvents, there is a possibility that the user may click again on the button which triggers the loop. You should prevent this either by disabling the button (as here) or by setting a flag so that the loop will not run again.

1 Declare a variable in the Declarations section of the form:
```
Dim CancelFlag as Boolean
```

2 For the button which starts the long process, add the following code:
```
CommandButton1.Enabled=False
CancelFlag=False
```

3 In the middle of the loop add:
```
DoEvents
If CancelFlag then
Exit Sub
CommandButton1.Enabled=True
End if
```

This example uses DoEvents to provide a Cancel button during a lengthy code loop.

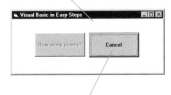

4 The code for the Cancel button is:
```
CancelFlag=True
```

Introducing Classes

See page 26 for more information about what methods are.

Visual Basic is called "object-based", because you treat items (like buttons and labels) as objects with properties that you can change and methods you can call. You can use the same technique with invisible or non-visual objects like databases.

Up until now, all the examples in this book have been about built-in objects. Visual Basic also makes it possible to define your own objects, for maximum flexibility.

There are several stages involved in making use of user-defined objects.

First, you define the object and the properties and methods it supports. The code that defines an object is called a Class. In Visual Basic, each class has its own code module, called a Class Module.

Next, you write code that creates a new object of the class you have defined. A class is not itself an object, but only defines an object. New objects are created at runtime using the Set statement.

Once the object has been created, you can use it in your code. You can create multiple objects of the same class. When an object goes out of scope, Visual Basic removes it from memory automatically.

See page 50 for more information about the scope of variables.

Creating visual objects

You can also create visual objects such as your own fancy buttons or customized list box. To create a visual object you need to create an ActiveX control. These are created as separate Visual Basic projects which you can then include in other applications you write. See Visual Basic's online help for more information about creating ActiveX controls.

Creating an ActiveX control in Visual Basic

Creating a Visual Basic Class

1 Start a new project and choose Project > Add Class Module.

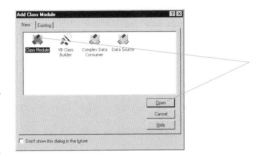

The VB Class Builder option opens a wizard that helps you create classes.
It is better to start without the wizard so that you learn what is involved.

2 From the Add Class Module dialog, select Class Module and click Open.

3 The new class module opens in a code window. With the code window selected, press F4 to show its properties. In the Name property type CPerson. Leave the other properties at the default value.

By convention, classes are named with an initial C. The example on the following pages uses a CPerson class to define a Person object.

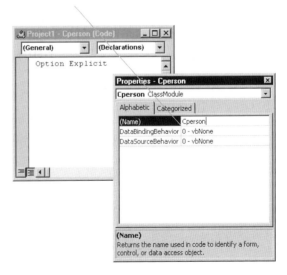

Defining and using a class

Adding a property to a class usually involves three elements. The current value of the property is usually stored in a private variable, visible only within the class itself. By convention, these are prefixed with the letter m. Next, two property procedures are added. Although there is only one property, there are separate procedures for reading and writing the property value. The advantage is that this gives you control over what values the property is allowed to have, and an opportunity to take some action when it changes.

1 To add a property to the new class, choose Tools>Add Procedure. From the dialog that appears, select Property and enter the name LastName. Then click OK.

You can make a property read-only by deleting the Property Let procedure and leaving only a Property Get procedure.

2 In the code window for the class module, two new property procedures appear. Add a private variable and code to read and write to it as shown here.

```
Project1 - Cperson (Code)
(General)                            LastName [PropertyLet]

Option Explicit

Private mLastName As String

Public Property Get LastName() As Variant
LastName = mLastName
End Property

Public Property Let LastName(ByVal vNewValue As Variant)
mLastName = vNewValue
End Property
```

You can have code that runs whenever an object is created from your class, for example to set initial property values. In the code window, find the Initialize event for the class and put the code there.

3 Next, add a method to display the property value to the user. Select Tools>Add procedure again, and this time choose Function. Call it ShowName and click OK.

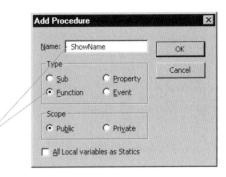

4 Display the form for the project by double-clicking Form1 in the Project Explorer, and add a button. In the Click event for the button add the following code:

```
Private Sub Command1_Click()
Dim person As Cperson
Set person = New Cperson
person.LastName = "Johnson"
person.ShowName
End Sub
```

There is a lot more to learn about classes, which are one of Visual Basic's most powerful features. See the online Programmer's Guide for more information.

5 Test your new class by running the application. When you click the button, Visual Basic creates a CPerson object, sets its LastName property, and calls the ShowName method.

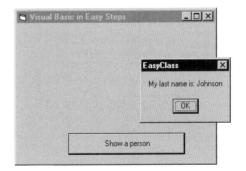

Where help files come from

Most professional software comes with help files. Press F1 in a dialog box, and custom help appears for that dialog.

Microsoft's help workshop is a tool to assist the management of old-style Windows help files.

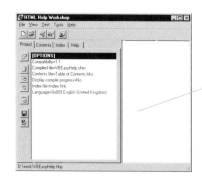

A new Microsoft tool, HTML help workshop, is for creating new-style HTML help like that used by Visual Basic itself from version 6.0.

There are two kinds of Windows help. The older kind uses files with an .hlp extension. To create these files, you would usually write the help in Microsoft Word, following certain special rules, and compile it to a help file using the Windows help compiler. The Help Workshop supplied with Visual Basic is a tool to assist the task.

The newer kind uses HTML files, as used for web pages, although these can also be compiled into a file with a .chm (compiled HTML) extension. Microsoft's HTML help workshop will help you create this kind of help.

Whichever you use, the final stage is to link the help file with your application. This is done in the Project Properties, and then by setting the HelpContextId property of individual forms and controls to match references in the help file.

The application's help file is specified in the Project Properties.

Using the Deployment Wizard

If you find the Package and Deployment Wizard hard to work with, investigate third-party alternatives such as InstallShield or WISE.

When you have completed a Visual Basic application, you will naturally want to distribute it to others. Unfortunately, installing a Windows application is not straightforward. The main reason is that applications use shared code libraries (called Dynamic Link Libraries) that may or may not already exist on the target system. These libraries are issued in different versions, to introduce improvements or fix bugs, so another problem is ensuring that the right version is installed. Overwriting a library file with an older version is a bad mistake.

ActiveX controls, in reality another kind of shared library, pose just the same problems, and introduce another of their own. To work, an ActiveX control must be registered, which means that details of its properties and methods are entered into a system database called the Registry.

Older versions of Visual Basic have an Application Setup Wizard that does the same job as the Deployment wizard, but works in a slightly different way.

All this means that you cannot just copy an application to a floppy disk, then copy it onto someone else's hard disk and expect it to work. Instead, you need to create a set of installation disks which include a setup application. This application does the work of checking versions, copying files, registering ActiveX controls, and finally installing program shortcuts onto the Start menu. Fortunately, Visual Basic has a wizard which will create this setup application for you. The following example demonstrates how this works with a simple application. It is the Interest Calculator created on page 55.

The Package and Deployment Wizard is an add-in. If it does not appear on your menu, install it using the Add-in manager.

Getting started

Having checked that your application is fault-free, compile and save it. Then choose Package and Deployment Wizard from the Add-ins menu.

Ensure you have some free disk space before running the Setup wizard. You will need room to create disk images for your application, as well as space for the wizard's temporary files.

2 Ensure the correct project is showing, and then click Package, to create a setup routine that can be run from floppy disks, CD, or across a network.

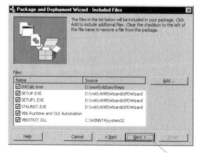

3 In the dialog that appears, select Standard Setup Package, and click Next.

4 You will be asked to choose where to create the setup package. The default is a subdirectory of your project folder and is a good choice. Click Next.

You should be very cautious about removing files that the wizard thinks are needed. Unless you know Windows through and through, it is hard to be sure about the "dependencies" – files that need other files to run.

5 The wizard lists the runtime files it detects are necessary for your application to run. The wizard cannot always detect every file used, so the Add button lets you add further files. In this case, no others are needed. Click Next to continue.

...cont'd

Only choose Multiple cabs if you intend to distribute the application on floppy disks. (1.44 MB is the size of standard floppy disks.)

6 Specify whether you want a single large install file, along with the setup application, or whether you need to split it to fit on floppy disks. Then click Next.

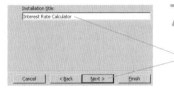

7 The next dialog lets you choose the title that appears when the setup runs. Type an appropriate title and click Next.

Test the Setup routine on several systems before releasing, including one that does not have Visual Basic already installed.

8 This dialog lets you set how the application appears on the user's Start menu. Click Properties to replace the default project name with a friendly version. Click OK and then Next.

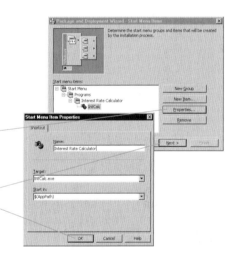

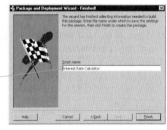

9 In the Install Locations and Shared files dialogs, simply click Next. Finally enter a Script name and click Finish.

10 Run Setup.exe to test the completed install routine.

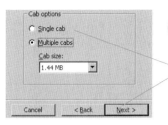

The setup wizard also creates an uninstall program. You can see this after running the setup, in the Add/ Remove Programs part of Control Panel.

Where next?

You have come to the end of *Visual Basic in easy steps*, but there is plenty more to learn and achieve. Here are some tips.

1. Start a project

It is hard to learn how to program if you have no clear goal. Find a project, whether at home, in the office, or at a club, and work out how to use Visual Basic to create a solution. Even if your first attempt is not completely successful, you will learn a lot by solving the real-world problems it throws up.

2. Get help

Whatever problem you have, the chances are that someone, somewhere has tackled it before. Because Visual Basic is so popular, you can easily find help in books and on the Internet. Microsoft run Internet newsgroups on Visual Basic, where you can ask questions.

3. Test and improve

In business, the customer is always right. In software, the user is always right. If your Visual Basic program is to be used by others, get them to try it out and report back the problems they have. Even better, watch them working and see how you can make the software more productive, by cutting down the number of steps needed to perform some task, or improving the screen layout, or speeding performance at critical points.

Visual Data Manager is itself a Visual Basic application. By studying the code for this and other sample applications, you can pick up great tips for your own projects.

Index